# THE GUEST HOUSE

Nancy,
I've been "held together" over the last 17 years thanks to you! I treasure our talks and your wisdom. You enrich my life.
Blessings always,
Jacqueline

# THE GUEST HOUSE

## A Journey of Discovery through Cancer

W. JACQUELINE JOHNSON

**THE GUEST HOUSE**
**A JOURNEY OF DISCOVERY THROUGH CANCER**



*iUniverse books may be ordered through booksellers or by contacting:*

*iUniverse*
*1663 Liberty Drive*
*Bloomington, IN 47403*
*www.iuniverse.com*
*1-800-Authors (1-800-288-4677)*



*ISBN: 978-1-4917-5055-1 (sc)*
*ISBN: 978-1-4917-5054-4 (e)*

*Library of Congress Control Number: 2014920265*

*Printed in the United States of America.*

*iUniverse rev. date: 11/10/2014*

*For my mother, who read to me every night when I was a child, sending me to sleep in an ocean of language.*

# TABLE OF CONTENTS

Introduction ..... ix

**Part One: Diagnosis**

1 Discovery ..... 3
2 The Surgeon ..... 5
3 Despite All, Happiness ..... 9
4 The Tumor Rears Its Ugly Head ..... 13
5 A Change in Plans ..... 16
6 The *Day* ..... 18

**Part Two: Treatment**

7 The Tumor Rears Its Ugly Head Again ..... 23
8 The Plot Thickens ..... 28
9 As I Wait ..... 33
10 Preparing to Be Hairless ..... 38
11 A Loss ..... 41
12 The Long Parade of Days ..... 43
13 Chemo Is Coming ..... 46
14 The Port ..... 48
15 I Become Toxic ..... 50
16 Changes ..... 52
17 How Would You Like to Go to Hollywood? ..... 58
18 The Gauze Pads Go, and So Does the Hair ..... 61
19 The Easter Season Is Upon Us ..... 65

20 The Second Infusion ... 69
21 Slowly the Days Go By ... 72
22 Nighttime, Flowers, and Pretzels ... 75
23 The Boston Bombings ... 77
24 Lessons ... 79
25 The Third Infusion ... 82
26 Marriage ... 85
27 The Last Infusion ... 88
28 The Next Step: Radiation ... 92
29 Meet the Kids ... 97
30 Hair Wisps ... 99
31 The World Beckons ... 100
32 Another Surgery ... 102
33 A Shift in Patients ... 103
34 I *Do* Have Lymphedema ... 104
35 I Am Radiated ... 106
36 Breath and Babies ... 108
37 Back in the Land of Getting Things Done ... 110
38 Reaction ... 113
39 Coming Back ... 115
40 A Death ... 117
41 Summer's End ... 119
42 Winding Down ... 122

**Part Three: Aftermath**

43 A Scare ... 127
44 Transformation ... 131

What Can You Do for a Friend Who Has Cancer? ... 133
Acknowledgments ... 135

# INTRODUCTION

Where does a journey begin? Perhaps there is no precise moment in the evolution of our being when a journey begins or ends but an ongoing thread emerging in the questions of our young years, circumventing the doubts and denials of early adulthood, and then reemerging on a clearer path over time.

This particular phase of my journey began with a pain in my thumb that had climbed up my arm, bidding for attention. My husband Dave and I were busy with our careers at the time, his in engineering, mine in teaching. Our children were in various stages of being launched into their own worlds: one in college, the other two living on their own. It had been a year of amazing synchronicity, and I had just returned from a retreat where I was encouraged to draw. Now, sitting on the floor next to our bed, I took up crayon and paper. What emerged was the figure of a robed woman sitting on the floor. "Weeping Woman" came as the title of the picture. "Why is she weeping?" I wrote. "She is weeping because she is broken. But you can heal her. Go to the IM School of Healing Arts." The pain disappeared.

Wow. I was supposed to become a healer. I immediately had fantasies of touching people who would be miraculously and gratefully healed. I enrolled in the school, and for the next five years, I traveled on weekends from our home in upstate New York to Manhattan. During my studies and experiences there, it became apparent that the woman who needed healing was me.

My education continued for another five years with the Raphaelite Healing Order. A question we often addressed had to do with the difference between curing and healing. The two words seem to be inexorably intertwined. Yet there are differences between them. Curing, I learned, happens when the symptoms of a disease or condition disappear. We see a doctor or surgeon or other medical professional in order to be cured. Healing, on the other hand might be described as the spirit part of the mind-body-spirit connection. It is an internal process, while curing is external. Healing involves shedding old ways that keep us tied to unhealthy patterns. Healing transforms us from our imagined, defended selves to who we truly are, ultimately awakening us to the divinity residing within. Curing *can* occur as we shed unhealthy memories, old grudges, or misconceptions through the healing process. Curing is finite, while healing transcends time.

Our culture informs us that we must fight our disease. We hear such phrases as "she fought bravely" or "he lost his battle." But what if, I queried as I studied, we join the disease, befriend it and learn from it?

I retired from teaching, which allowed me to study and freed me to live a more contemplative life. I was happy and healthy, needing no medications and very few visits to the doctor. Dave and I lived in a hillside home overlooking a lake, a setting we'd dreamed of on our first date. Life was good. I was grateful for all the knowledge and wisdom my teachers had given me. But soon I was to enter another phase of my journey, meeting the most demanding and exacting teacher of all: cancer.

What happened next challenged all I had learned about healing and changed me in ways I never could have imagined. This is my story.

# PART ONE

## DIAGNOSIS

# DISCOVERY

"I can't believe you have cancer," my daughter says, her fingers curling tightly over a mug of tea.

"Me either," I reply quietly. I welcome the warmth of the cup against my fingers, even though it is early summer. Suzanne, our youngest, is tall and slim like her father. She shares many of his characteristics except a rapier wit, my contribution to her inheritance. She wears her forty-two years lightly, I think, looking at her wrinkle-free skin and wonderful figure.

Not wanting to upset her or her brothers—Todd, who lives on the west coast, and Kyle in Pennsylvania—I had been nervous about telling our kids I had a malignant breast tumor. Moreover, I felt that by being diagnosed with cancer, I had made a mistake somewhere along the way. Having cancer was a bad thing, making me suspect a careless person. How could I have let this happen to me?

"I mean, no one in our family has had cancer," Suzanne continues. "Well, almost." She is referring to Todd, our oldest, who has had testicular cancer.

"Yes," I answer vaguely, taking in the beauty of our property: late-blooming flowers, endless lawns, and pastures that stretch for a mile down to a long, slim lake. I am so grateful for my life here, for my daughter who lives nearby, for our close relationship. "Yes," I repeat more firmly. "He was lucky." *Will I be as lucky?*

My neighbor was responsible for the detection, perhaps for saving my life. After showering one day, I happened to glance in the mirror that sat on the bathroom counter. What I saw was a reflection of the side of my breast, a place I could not have seen except from that position. The skin was crinkly. I would have put it down to old lady fat had my neighbor not have seen something similar, something that turned out to be a malignancy. I called my doctor.

What followed was standard procedure but new to me. First, I had a mammogram. Following that, an ultra sound was performed, and then a biopsy was administered. A young student nurse accompanied me as I left the radiology department. "Good luck," she said with a reassuring smile. *This is nothing,* I thought. *The tumor will turn out to be benign.*

It didn't.

# THE SURGEON

It is morning. As I wake, I slowly remember. *I have this thing in me. It can't really be felt and is quiet. It doesn't hurt. Yet it has the potential to kill me.*

I have cancer. But I *will not* be afraid. I will not run away, and I will not fight. I will join the cancer and see what it has to teach me. Cancer is an opportunity to heal, and I welcome this opportunity.

Today is my visit to the surgeon, the first of what will turn out to be many doctor visits. My trusty sidekick David will accompany me. His tall frame and blue eyes suggest a calm demeanor, but he is not as placid as he looks. Usually, his mind is a racetrack of ideas, plans, and solutions to problems. Highly creative and talented, he is often a guy in jeans and an old shirt, puttering around the house and property. Today, however, he is as uncertain as I am. I chose this surgeon carefully, consulting my most valuable resource, a nurse. He comes highly recommended. "He is very skilled as a surgeon and extremely compassionate," my nursing friend says, giving him thumbs-up approval.

Although he has a kind face and speaks softly, he is not very compassionate this morning. "I've been looking for your records, and I had a devil of a time finding them. Apparently it is not Jacqueline but W. Jacqueline. Why do people mess with their names?" he grumbles.

Oh, no, the name thing. As a two-year-old I had changed my name from Wanda Jacqueline to a shorter Baby Jac. From then on, my family called me Jac. Wanda became a foreign name, a hated appendage that was not me. I finally replaced it with a W that sits inconspicuously in front of Jacqueline. *Should I tell him about this? I think not.*

I sit facing him, feeling very small. Even the sight of David, my husband of over fifty years and chief supporter, does not help. The surgeon gets right down to business. "The tumor is slightly too large for a lumpectomy. I prefer not to perform a mastectomy because it is too invasive," he continues, visibly outlining what a mastectomy involves.

Terrified, I squeak out a reply: "I second that plan!"

"What we can do is shrink the tumor with chemotherapy." Everything in me says *no.* Chemotherapy is deadly, a primitive treatment in a modern world. I have said I would never agree to be treated with chemo, so we go to plan B, which is to shrink the tumor with a hormone-inhibiting pill, since it is hormone-sensitive.

"I suggest you get a notebook to keep records of all your treatments, particularly medications. You'll be dealing with several doctors, and you need to keep on top of that," he says, leaning against the wall and crossing his arms. This is his turf. He's delivered this talk hundreds of times. But I'm a newbie, and I feel overwhelmed. Yet I am grateful that he agrees to hormone treatment.

As we leave the office, I turn to Dave. "I feel as if I'd been hit by a bus."

To soothe our shock, Dave and I stop at the hospital gift shop across from the surgeon's office, a practice I started after the biopsy. David is patient with me as I buy sandals and a ring. Next, we head to Starbucks, a place we call our trauma center. Both do little to change a dull ache in the pit of my stomach.

"We are entering into a totally different reality," Dave says as we drive home. I look through the windshield at the beautiful sky and intricate cloud formations. *Could this be possible?* I wonder. How little I knew then.

I imagine my tumor getting smaller. My thoughts center on the word *shrink.* I tell very few people about my diagnosis, and when I do, I refer to it as a malignant tumor, not cancer.

I buy a bright pink notebook and put in paper. At the front, I put in a copy of a poem by Rumi that I hope to be my talisman.

> This being human
> is a guest house,
> every morning a new arrival.
> A joy, a depression, a meanness,
> some momentary awareness.
> Welcome and entertain them all!
> Even if they are a crowd of sorrows
> who violently sweep your house
> empty of its furniture,
> still treat each guest honorably.
> He may be clearing you out for
> some new delight.
> The dark thought, the sham,
> the malice,
> meet them at the door laughing
> and invite them in.
> Be grateful for whoever comes,
> because each has been sent
> as a guide from beyond.

# DESPITE ALL, HAPPINESS

Starlings have gathered in the tall pines across the street, their chattering an undercurrent of constant sound. Like me, they are waiting. For the first time, I've allowed myself to feel frightened, an uncharacteristic reaction for me. As I walk in the fields behind our house, I realize that although I am afraid, I can deal with it. I ask the Virgin Mary for her love and support, as well as for her courage, faith, and strength to flow through me. I realize that I need to be a container as well as a channel for healing. I wish to embody the grace of acceptance.

It is another day of quiet except for the distant hum of a lawn mower. On this luscious green and gold day, I feel that everything will be okay, wondrous, extraordinary. I still try to get in touch with my feelings, which is difficult to do today. I want to recognize what I feel, to honor my feelings and deal graciously with whatever comes up.

Suzanne calls, saying she needs to talk. She sounds "down," so I put on the kettle and check our wine supply. When she arrives, she asks me to help her get something out of her car. I accompany her and stop. Belted in the passenger seat is the biggest, fattest teddy bear ever. "Oh, my goodness!" I exclaim.

"He's your Care Bear," she sings happily as she puts him in my arms.

"Oh, Suzanne, thank you. I'd give you a hug, but..." We laugh, realizing that his bulk prevents it. "I'll name him al Fattah, which means 'the opener of the way.'" Cancer, I believe, will open the way for me.

Summer and early fall go by, and I act as if nothing is wrong. In September, we go to Moyersville, Pennsylvania, to celebrate grandson Andrew's ninth birthday. Andrew and Eddie, Kyle's sons, are the joy of my life. Andrew's bone structure and eyes are very much like those in our family. He reminds me of my father. The difference is Andrew's skin color, tawny in the winter and walnut in the summer, like his South American ancestors. Eddie, eighteen months younger, looks very much like his Brazilian family; only his fair skin shows our northern ancestry.

Our daughter-in-law Clarisse has been running many miles, practicing for a half-marathon. She has the body of a runner, slim and firm. A talented woman, she does well at whatever she turns her hand to, so I expect she will do well in the marathon. On Sunday, the big day, we accompany her to the town where the race begins. We drop her off near the starting point, and as she slips out of the van, she says, "This one's for you, Jackie." Clarisse is not given to spoken sentiments, so I am not only stunned but deeply touched by her statement. I begin to cry. We drive past police vehicles whose blinking lights blend into a shrieking strobe. Volunteers put up barriers and set up cones, marking a path for the runners. I see this through a blur of tears. I've recovered by the time we pull into Perkin's parking lot for breakfast, but after we travel to the vicinity of the race, tears begin once again.

As we watch the runners, I, who rarely cry, silently sob behind my sunglasses. They arrive one by one, some winded, others running and breathing easily. We stretch, looking for Clarisse, who finally comes into view looking fresh as a daisy, having completed what she thought was a thirteen-kilometer half marathon but what she discovered (en route) was actually thirteen miles. At the finish line, I hug her and sob. "I thought of you through the whole race, and you just pulled me along," she says, "just as you will be pulled along in your race—and you will win it."

There is an air of triumph in that small city square at the finish line. People mill about, talking and eating fruit from stands bursting with color. A band plays. David and Andrew begin to dance. I look up into the blue September sky. Above the chaotic scene, a lone monarch butterfly floats effortlessly. This picture lodges in my brain, an image of hope.

The September skies have been spectacular. One sunset stands out: rays of light coming down through the clouds and then shooting upward, tipping them with liquid gold. All this reflects my mood: deep, incredible happiness as I drive to visit my friend Patrice, a cancer survivor.

A warm and giving yet stoic woman, she has been a good friend for many years. Drinking tea with Patrice has become tradition. As she fills my cup, we talk. "I am not telling people I have cancer but say I have a malignant tumor," I reveal, selecting a cookie from an attractive arrangement on the table before me.

She eyes me, takes a sip of tea, and answers in her no-nonsense way, "You have cancer."

# THE TUMOR REARS ITS UGLY HEAD

In November, I have an MRI to check the size of the tumor, a procedure I think will be no big deal. Yet as we get closer to the hospital, my body turns to jelly. A technician prepares to draw blood but has such a tough time that an "expert" is called in. My veins seem to be resisting. I don't blame them.

I approach the big machine and am told to lie face down, putting my breasts into little cups—another female indignity. I say something about this and am told the machine was designed by a man. Go figure. I am moved into a tight enclosure open at both ends, a round coffin of terrible sounds: beeps, bleeps, rat-a-tat-tats, clicks, clacks: all loud. I am wearing earphones. The people in charge are in another room and can talk to me through a microphone. I can reply but not initiate any conversation. If I am in trouble, I have to wave my feet. They have to be kidding! I recite mantras all the time I am in the enclosure.

They wheel me out, and I sit up shakily. "Do I get a lollipop?" I ask.

"You get a whole bag," the technician replies.

Dave has been waiting just outside the room. "Definitely Starbucks," I say.

But we change our minds and instead drive out into the chill wind, heading home. Leaves sail across the pavement. The risk takers soar to unbelievable heights and play with the currents. November: newly skeletal trees, their remaining leaves of amber, brown, and gold adding soft autumn color. Cornstalks in uncut fields rattle their unique tune, and low bushes dot the landscape with deep burgundy.

There is a feel about November: a coming together, a gathering of quilts, and a comfort of warm socks. We return home to a fire in the wood stove and tea so hot it makes my glasses steam.

Everywhere is quiet. There is little wind today. All I can hear is the starlings gathering in the giant old trees across the street. Their mutterings sound like musical chewing. Cancer has made a difference in my life. I can center on each task. Time seems different. When I do get upset about something, I stop and ask, *How important is this? Do I really want to think this way?* I seem to be floating from one event to the next.

Last night, I went into a deep, deep sleep. Near morning, I heard or sensed a voice saying, "You are surrounded by love." It is the most wonderful feeling—like I am in a little boat floating on an ocean of love.

Things keep changing. I feel as if we're at a tennis match and I'm the ball. I walk outside and ask for guidance. What I get is an urge to walk our labyrinth and then write in my journal. Not able to think of anything to say, I do a ten-minute write. I survey the several choices facing me: surgery, chemotherapy, and hormone shrinkage. After silently deliberating, I come to a conclusion. Perhaps surgery might be my best option.

As I write, I am calm. Is this a sign of spiritual maturity, or is it denial?

The final decision is to go with hormone blockage for twelve weeks, check, and then do surgery. I continue taking Lexotrole (Femara). But what is going on inside?

Had I known the answer to this question, I might have made different choices.

# A CHANGE IN PLANS

Another MRI is scheduled to check the size of the tumor. This time, I go prepared with earplugs, which I wear along with headphones. I still feel as if I'm in the middle of a battlefield. We have a break between appointments, so we head for Starbucks and then return for test number two, an ultrasound to see if the tumor really is shrinking. The technician takes forever, probing here and there. Finally, she leaves, and I lie on the table shivering until she finally returns. It seems she has discovered another tumor behind the first one. I am led on shaky legs to the mammography department to have another mammogram. Shrinking the tumor is no longer an option. As I leave the hospital after an entire day of tests, I remember the cheery wish of good luck from last summer.

My luck is not good.

Surgery is scheduled for January. I go through Christmas surrounded by nieces Anne and Mary, grandkids Andrew and Eddie, Kyle, Todd, Suzanne and Paul, her partner. The house bulges with their happy presence. Nothing is said about cancer, about upcoming surgery. We eat, drink, play games, and frolic in the snow that has made this a perfect Christmas. Mary brings a bottle of Bailey's Irish Cream, which we polish off. I buy another after Christmas and have a drink nightly as I wait for *the day.*

# THE *DAY*

My surgery time is early morning. We arrive in the January dark and slowly mount stairs to the surgery unit. While I feel okay now, it will be a long time before I will be able to look at these steps without a sense of dread. I check in and sit down with Dave. "I can't believe I'm this centered," I say, slipping my hand in his. He smiles and squeezes my hand. I wonder what emotions hide behind his benevolent exterior.

An older man with a cane approaches, asks if he can pray with us, and explains where things are: bathrooms, cafeteria. I hear steps on the stairs, and Zaynab, my dear friend and spiritual counselor, arrives. "Hello. How are you doing?" I hug her, welcoming her special warmth, her calm cheerfulness. Zaynab is my saint in beautiful shoes, her passion. Today she looks as chic as ever, a jaunty scarf accenting her outfit.

"I'm okay," I answer bravely, even feeling a truth in the statement. Then my name is called, and I rise like an actress called onstage. I sweep through the door of the prep and recovery rooms, where I am hospital gowned and marked for surgery: right side for the plastic surgeon, who will perform a breast reduction, and left for the other surgeon, who will perform the mastectomy. I have opted for surgical implants and plan to leave here with a new chest. Through all of this, I am in a state of self-induced calm. There is no more denial or pretending. This is the real deal. Suzanne arrives and is, as always, a bright light. I've seen both surgeons and the anesthesiologist, who surprises me by wearing make-up and earrings, not the usual medical garb. The sides of my gurney are clicked up, a final sound. Zaynab leans over the side and prays:

> "Beloved Lord, almighty God,
> through the rays of the sun,
> the waves of the air,
> through the all-pervasive life in space,
> purify and revivify Jacqueline
> and, I pray, heal her body, heart and soul."

I am kissed, wished well, and wheeled away.

# PART TWO

## TREATMENT

# THE TUMOR REARS ITS UGLY HEAD AGAIN

Sleep. People hover around me. Voices. I come up slowly from a long cavern. "How do you feel?" The voices belong to people: nurses, Dave, Suzanne, Zaynab, and Cheryl, who has joined the crew and gives me socks that are pink for cancer awareness. I'm only too aware of cancer right now. I think I'm doing just fine, but Suzanne tells me later that I had a terrible time. The day passes into early evening, and the nurses tell me I must go home, even though I keep insisting I should stay in the hospital. I leave in the dark holding a pink carnation that thanks me for choosing that hospital. *Choosing?* I think wearily. *I didn't choose any of this.*

Suzanne has gone on ahead and fixed our lounge chair with flannel sheets and a cozy blanket. I cannot sleep in a bed, as I have drainage tubes and have to be careful not to roll on them. My friend Eileen, a nurse, has come to sleep on the couch next to me, just in case. Eileen comes from a large

German Catholic family, and her ethics are grounded in hard work and obedience. These, coupled with her gift for compassion, make her an excellent nurse. Our backgrounds couldn't be more diverse, yet we've been close friends for years, following each other's spiritual paths, listening, and offering mutual support.

I sleep well and wake to notice a dead mouse on the floor. *Oh, no, I don't want Eileen to see it.* I think sanitation. Gia, the cat, slinks into the room and begins to play with the corpse. She tosses it high in the air, and for a terrible second, I think it will land on me. But it doesn't, and Eileen never notices the creature.

My recovery goes well, even seeming swift. Suzanne and I go for short walks when the weather is nice. If I overdo, I'm again confined to the blanketed lounge chair for rest and comfort. Friends stop in, and we eat soup on the winter evenings. But things don't turn out exactly as I'd hoped. The tumor was nastier than anyone could have imagined. The pathologist reported that it had looped around and grown behind itself. Not only that, but it hadn't been content to stay in one place. "I removed twenty-five lymph nodes," reports the surgeon. "Twenty-four of them were infected. I've never seen such a large number."

There is a word for this: metastases. This is a dreaded word, and it ramps my cancer involvement to stage 3A. It is serious. Has the cancer gone further? I am too shocked to feel fear, to feel anything. Moreover, I didn't have the reconstruction surgery, as the plastic surgeon thought things were not quite ready. The other surgeon disagreed, but he wasn't the one calling the shots. My chest is only half new and lopsided.

It rains so hard the TV image shuts down. The strange weather only adds to my mood. The next part of my journey will be recovery and attack. Attack means chemotherapy. I feel trapped. I hadn't researched other avenues of treatment, and I'm too weak to do it now. It seems as if there is no other path. Surgery, chemotherapy, and radiation are the shining sisters of cancer treatment, and I go along with this, albeit reluctantly.

The wound from my surgery is reddish at one end. I check it out with the surgeon, who says "You have an infection. I'll have to go in and clean this up." I don't say anything but wrinkle my nose. "Don't wrinkle your nose," the surgeon snaps. *Don't wrinkle my nose? Don't wrinkle my nose? He wants me to go back in for dreaded surgery, and he tells me not to wrinkle my nose*? His rating on the compassionate scale slips down several notches.

Three days before the surgery, I have a PET scan to see if the cancer has metastasized further. PET is short for Position Emission Tomography, with concurrently acquired computed tomography. The test is performed in a nearby city. I am greeted by a team of jolly people. "What does W stand for?" one inquires.

"What?"

"What does W stand for? Your name appears as W Johnson and we've been dying to know what W would look like. We didn't even know if you would be a man or a woman."

Oh, good grief, the name thing again! We all have a good laugh, and I am fed barium (which now smells and tastes like piña colada), injected with a radioactive isotope attached to glucose molecules, and told to rest under heated blankets in a darkened room. After an hour, my body is x-rayed. The glucose molecules from the injection seek out active cells, such as busily growing cancer cells. Since cancer cells show up as a different light, the radiologist can tell just where they are in my body. "These images will be in your doctor's office before you leave here," the technician tells me, proud of this complicated procedure. "You'll be radioactive for three hours, so you must stay at least three feet away from other people and pets. If you use the toilet, flush two times." I ride home in the back seat of the car.

On a gray, nondescript day, David and I drive in to the cancer center to get the results of my PET scan. Only small patches of snow remain on the dead landscape; the houses we pass are bleak. I feel every bump in the road as if the car has square wheels. *With so many lymph nodes involved, the cancer could easily be in other places. Couldn't it?* I do a mental checklist of my organs, imagining the worst.

By the time we reach the oncologist's office, I am emotionally dead. The door opens, and he breezes in, young, agile, a broad smile on his face. He reaches out with his hand to shake mine, saying, "The scan was negative." I stare at him, too dumbfounded to speak. "Did you hear me?" he repeats. "The scan is negative."

# THE PLOT THICKENS

Today, the surgeon does cutting and pasting to edit my wound. In recovery, I discover heated hospital gowns. Air is pumped into the gown, much like those old hairdryers that pumped air into a turban on one's head. "Imagine being this comfortable after surgery," I muse.

"Come on, Jacqueline, time to go home," the nurse insists while I wail that I'm too comfortable to move.

I have a yucky open wound that has a strange dressing involving a rope that somehow absorbs the infection. "I'm assigning you a visiting nurse to help change the dressing until Dave gets the hang of it," my surgeon says when he comes to check on me following surgery.

"What do you think?" I ask Dave. He just smiles.

Medicare has me on house arrest. Seriously: I can't go anywhere. Because I am now a patient of home care, I am considered to be housebound. I will have a visiting nurse who comes every other day to change my dressing. On Sunday, the intake nurse comes. She is a comfortable woman, soft-spoken and kind as she asks different questions. Then the nurse inspects the house and gives me many precautions about falling. She is not happy with the throw rugs on the floor. "I want you to be in the best possible place for your good health," she assures me. "You must never be alone. If David is in the yard, you both must have your cell phones. We are here for you. Feel free to call any time." Her directions are interspersed with incidents she has shared with a friend who had cancer. It is a good friend, I surmise. I also suspect that the friend has died.

"You need to build your body up, so eat lots of protein. Peanut butter is okay." I cheer. Then she surprises me by asking me how I feel about what is happening to me. No one has asked me that. I show her a card I have received. She reads the message and looks up. "What a beautiful message. You are lucky to have such friends."

"I am," I reply. "Not only that, but I have received flowers. Cancer has taught me that I am valued, and I hope it will teach me many more things. I hope this experience will change me."

She packs up her things to leave and then says, "Can I give you a hug?" We hug, and she cries.

Sun shines on the snow, creating sparkles. It's warm enough for a walk later on, but for now, I enjoy winter from indoors.

Deer tracks in the snow attest to the fact that they must have been having fun in our back yard. It might be some kind of convention, or perhaps a contest to see who can nuzzle down to the most grass.

I could look at this time as a crashing bore, as I am so limited in what I can do. But I choose to look at it as time to enjoy rest and inspect the inner landscape. Our property, called Quiet Meadows, is in a beautiful spot. We have lived here for over fifty years, and its peace is in our bones. I have a new nurse now, a woman with masses of auburn hair. She wears it caught up, but some spills over in saucy curls. "How are you doing?" she asks.

I sigh. "I am completely content to just be here," I answer.

"I don't blame you," she says, looking around at the snowscape outdoors, the crackling fire within. "I could do that."

Although I have been sleeping reasonably well, one night I dream that a parking lot has been built over my left breast and someone is placing four large vehicles in that parking lot. I wake up feeling like four large vehicles *have* been placed on my chest. My first thought is to wish I could just not feel any pain for a while. Then, after taking an aspirin, I settle back and think this is a great time to practice *tonglen. Tonglen,* a Tibetan practice, teaches us to let in suffering and offer our compassion. My suffering, rarely more than a five on the pain scale, is small. Yet I am in a position to understand suffering, not run from it. Being there allows me to experience others and their suffering in a way I otherwise could not. Thus, my heart opens, and I am a part of a greater existence. This is a teaching. This is a gift.

I am reminded that being cured is a combination of inner and outer work, the outer part being good diet, exercise, and medication. My visiting nurse reminds me that pain gets in the way of healing, so I fall back on narcotics and take a pain pill. I have the best sleep in several nights. I must remember that some medications are good for the body.

The sun is out. What a joy the sun is, warming and illuminating everything it touches. This is God's smile as well as his blessing. On this sunny day, I'm thinking about love. I'm learning to love my body more, especially *the wound.* My left breast is probably wondering what it ever did to deserve the treatment it has been given. So I send it my love.

Years ago, I was assigned to observe a teacher who was on probation because of complaints about his treatment of students. I really didn't care for the man. I sat in his class every day for forty-two minutes. I sat and sat. What could I do with this time? I began to pray for him. I prayed for that man for forty-two minutes every day. Gradually, I began to see him as a person. While his teaching techniques weren't stellar, he wasn't mean. I even began to like him more. When I was assigned to his class, I offered to sit down and talk with him about his teaching, but he had flatly refused. Finally, one day, he stopped me after class, *took my hands in his,* and suggested we talk about his class and ways I could help while I was there. I was so touched by the experience that when I got home, I cried.

Unfortunately, he was let go that very day. Each of his observers was asked to write a report about his class. I wrote an anecdotal report, which was what the situation called for. He phoned me some days later to tell me mine was the only report that was not negative and thanked me. What happened? Love happened. Prayer is a form of love, and love performs miracles.

# AS I WAIT

The wound is too deep to be quickly cured. I feel okay except for this net contraption I wear across my chest to keep the dressing in place, as my skin is too raw to use more tape. I am beginning to feel trapped. There's not much to see outside in this rural landscape. Today, the snow drifts lazily from a pewter sky. Looking again, I notice the ballet of birds. They float down from the trees and angle for a place at the feeder. Or they dive-bomb straight to the ground and peck away at fallen seeds. The feeders can be full of birds, and all of a sudden, as if a conductor had lifted a baton, they scatter and disappear. Sometimes, that act is lifesaving. Every now and then, a merlin shows up and snatches a hapless bird. Merlins have to eat, too, Dave reminds me. This is the way nature works.

I am noticing nature more and more. Some days, the snow spills down in great, fluffy flakes, making me feel cozy. On such days, I sit by the fire, read, and drink tea. Other days, the pearl sky stretches on and on, no break in the color, just one continuous cloud. On such days, I feel sad.

When the temperature rises, the pristine snow melts and becomes dirty, sticking up in black spikes near the road. When I was seven, I tripped and fell while chasing another student. A piece of dirty snow sliced into my knee, making a deep cut that became infected. I still have the scar.

Friends come to the rescue during this long February. On David's birthday, Suzanne comes laden with an iron pot and groceries. After peeling, cutting, scraping, and searing, she produces a lovely birthday treat. On another day Lola, shows up with hot soup and Starbucks coffee, also hot. She also lends us a huge basket of DVDs. Cheryl brings heaps of flowers, welcome color that she helps me arrange. Eileen helps David load up wood and transport it to the porch. She and Dave cook dinner and we watch *Downton Abbey* on TV.

I'm in between doctor visits. It is wonderful being in town. There's so much to see. Wind is beginning to sculpt the snow, making delicate curves that decorate the roadside. People hurry about their tasks bundled up. It was fourteen degrees when we left home this morning with a wind chill of minus two. Our town trucks, ever vigilant, move back and forth along the highway, spitting salt onto the pavement. I wonder if they know something we don't. We go to Starbucks and then drive with our coffee to the nearby lake, where we watch cold, choppy water and seagulls resting on what is left of the ice. One gull assigns itself to our car, waiting hopefully and in vain for a treat.

I think he is the front man for the flock. His persistence reminds me of our black cat Gia, who can wait forever for a mouse.

The road crews did know something that we didn't. A storm comes, first as freezing rain, then snow, then more snow. We hurry around preparing for the possibility of downed power lines. We make sure no dirty dishes are in the dishwasher and store water to drink and water to use for everything else. No electricity means there isn't any water when one is on a well; ergo, one cannot drink, wash, or flush.

I'm glad to be inside my winter cocoon. The wind becomes vicious and tears chunks of snow from trees and bushes, sending it off in blizzard swirls. Clouds of ground snow rise heavenward like angels in a frenzied dance. Gia runs to the door, anxious to go out. But when I open it, she shrinks back and stays inside.

I'm still sufficiently tired to spend time in front of the TV. Tonight I watch a documentary on combat rescue, a program that holds fascination for me, reminding me of my childhood interest in war stories. Seeing this, I can understand how a young person could want to be in the military, especially in this branch of service. There are many aspects that astonish me: the speed of rescue, the danger of a helicopter putting down in the middle of enemy fire, the expertise of young medics who quickly patch up and make the injured ready for transport.

Then something happens that stops me in my tracks. A critically injured Special Forces soldier is loaded onto the waiting chopper. The narrator says, "There is a special tradition that when a critically injured soldier is taken out, the men in his unit kiss him before sending him off to treatment." This action left me dumbfounded. I was brought up in the forties, when men kissing one another or even showing anything less than *dealing with it* was unheard of. I had a view of the military as being macho, wary of physical contact.

Yet one by one, these burly men swathed in desert dusty combat gear step up, say a few words, and tenderly kiss their fallen comrade. How beautiful this moment is, touching me deeply and affirming my belief in healing. The wounded soldier lived and was sent home. Amen. Amen.

Yesterday morning, the eastern sky blazed with color: orange to coral to red. Not content with staying on the horizon, some pinks broke away and mounted clouds coming from the west, making a canopy of color over our road. The sun was hopeful this morning, turning everything it touched to pink gold. But then it paled, late winter warmth that utterly failed. I am the sun today, a burst of welcome energy followed by waves of exhaustion. This, perhaps, is my winter Hades: a time of wound and repair, a time of deep rest and welcome awakening, my winter in the underworld. Like Persephone, I hope to rise up with spring and return.

I'm trying to read my body's signals, an interesting exercise. When does my body want to eat? When should I rest? What, besides pills, will ease the discomfort on my chest? Sometimes it's obvious when I've gone too far, and I rush for the nearest surface to lie down or run to the kitchen for a snack. But I'm trying to get the clues before that happens. I have the feeling that our bodies are always talking to us, but it's so easy to do what we want and ignore the signs that they are no longer heard.

# PREPARING TO BE HAIRLESS

Although I haven't begun chemotherapy, I want to be prepared for hair loss, so today I enter the wonderful world of a little shop that caters to mastectomy needs. It is located in what was once a residence and still looks like one. I was told to enter from the rear of the building, so Dave parks, and I ring the doorbell of a locked door and wait. I look at David, and he looks at me. "What do you think?" I ask. Before he can answer, the door opens, and we enter a grotto-like interior and are led down a long, sinuous hall. The front room and desk are located amidst a cacophony of furniture. "I'm in the market for a wig," I tell the woman behind the desk.

"Of course," she replies and leads us into a small room that is just as packed with merchandise as the rest of the store. "Lily will be right with you," she chirps and leaves. I've done my homework and looked at wigs on their website. I have a list.

Lily enters, looking confused. "I usually don't work in wigs," she says, patting her hair. I hand her my list and smile. She runs down the paper. "Oh, dear, we don't have that in stock. That one is no longer available. We have this other one, but it's in the wrong color."

I'm not too fussy about color, but I had my shot at being blonde, and women in their seventies definitely should not go with black. Lily starts pulling boxes off the shelf and pawing through them. All of a sudden, she holds one up. "I'll try that one," I say hopefully.

She pulls a stocking over my hair. "Hey, you could pull that over your face and rob a bank," Dave says. I glare at him but then laugh. He is being very patient, and I'm glad he's with me. I try it on. Lily stands back and coos. It's not quite my color of gray, but it is perky.

"Your natural hair color is so lovely," Lily says, sensing my hesitation. I thank her while I think about my pewter-gray hair. *It will come back*, I pray. *Won't it?*

I find some hats: a newsboy cap with glitter, a soft black cap, and a little warm cap to wear at bedtime. I then pay, a process that takes forever. "You must think we don't know what we're doing," twitters the sweet lady. I smile. The transaction finally completed, we are led once again to the back door, which she unlocks. "Good luck," she calls as she disappears behind the door, clicking the lock.

"One day at a time," I answer to the empty air and push all the future away except for the lunch that awaits us at a favorite restaurant.

# A LOSS

Our dear friend Ann Hennessey has passed away, or died, or...what words does one use to describe the final passage? I prefer to say "passed into," for I do believe she has gone to a different place. Now I'm dealing with the fact that a close friend, a woman I've known since the midsixties when we taught preschool together, is no longer available to me here on earth. Ann, her husband Rich, and their children have been close friends with our family through trips to the Adirondacks, shared dinner parties, a trip to Ottawa's winter fest, hiking jaunts, enjoying local festivals, and concerts. We celebrated each New Year's Eve together, creating parties that included the children. Our boys stayed at their house when Suzanne was born, and they are her godparents.

Part of me says, "This couldn't be. Surely she was as immortal as our friendship. How could she be reduced to a mound of memories?"

Yet another part of me says with quiet acceptance, "It is her time. Death releases her from the terrible clutches of Alzheimer's, and she is free of the denseness of life." I celebrate her passing as much as I celebrate her rich life. Memories of Ann are precious jewels, and the love we shared as friends weaves about me, knowing no end, becoming a part of my being. She will always remain as close to me as the day I sat in her living room, petting her cat, when suddenly his tail came off in my hand. "Anne," I said in astonishment, "Your cat's tail just came off in my hand!" I held it up for her to see. The two of us stared at the hapless object, speechless. Then we both collapsed in laughter. (It seems the cat's tail had been caught in the door two days ago.) Oh, Ann, my dear friend, how I miss you.

# THE LONG PARADE OF DAYS

In this long parade of days while I wait for my wound to heal, Sunday stands out as being different. I remember, as a baby, sitting in my high chair in our kitchen, watching Grandmother and Mother flutter about with the preparation of a big meal. It is a gray day, and the windows are steamy. I sense the difference of the day. Somehow, I know it is Sunday. I feel that way today. There is little break in our routine, but there is the sense of liberation from chores and problems to solve, the slower pace. Moreover, all doctor's offices are closed. The *wound* continues to improve. Yesterday, I had no discomfort and felt more like myself than I have in a long time. Characteristically, I'm back to lots of discomfort today, as well as lower energy. Getting better is like our weather: unpredictable and swinging from one stage to the next.

Monday dawns as a morning of crystal snowflakes. Wind sweeps down over the field, bows, and asks the snow to dance. Accepting this invitation, snow falls into the wind's arms and swirls round and round, her skirts flying in great arches. I'm lucky enough to be in the kitchen at 7:45, so I can watch as our neighbor Johnny boards the school bus to go to kindergarten. Johnny is tiny. He stands at road's edge, looking up for the driver's signal that it's safe to cross. He bounces across the street, stepping way up on the high steps into the bus. Johnny is wearing a backpack that is one third as big as he is. What on earth could a kindergartner carry in his backpack? Our kids went off to kindergarten empty-handed.

Watching Johnny, I am aware of the flow of life. The earlier bus riders from *back in the day* are now parents and grandparents. We have a rock in our garden called the school bus rock. Our kids stood on that rock while waiting for the bus. When Kyle got old enough to appreciate the height of trees, he waited for the bus amidst the branches of our silver maple. In Suzanne's senior year, she had to walk all the way to the top of the road and wait. Her hair, wet from the shower, froze in the winter, and I imagine she had to thaw out at school. Todd was lucky. He had an old car during his senior year and drove the seven miles to school.

Life flows. We move from stage to stage, our familiar routines now memory. Once friends sat around the table drinking coffee as we shared anecdotes about our little children in conversations never finished because of mommy interruptions. Our thoughts are different now, perhaps more sad and deeper. We do get to finish each sentence, but even though we are older, tougher, and wiser, we are still trying to understand our place in the order of things.

# CHEMO IS COMING

There is a sense of expectancy in the hushed, pale atmosphere of this Monday. Perhaps plants are beginning to stir underground, to come away from their long sleep, twisting and stretching, aiming for the light. I, too, feel as if I am beginning to awaken from the aftermath of two surgeries. At night, in the dark shadows of pain, I wonder if this ever will be over. During the day, felled by exhaustion, I try to remember what normal feels like. But there is that moment when I realize the pain isn't there. It comes back again, but that prick of light is like the expectant atmosphere of this morning. I am getting better.

On Monday, the doctor's offices are open. I see my oncologist for the first time in weeks. He is cheerful. "By Thursday, the wound should be closed, and we can think about getting chemotherapy started. You'll need to have a port put in because your veins are too weak to withstand the chemo injections. I'm going to take you into the chemo infusion room so you can get acquainted."

He leads me into a cheery room lit by floor to ceiling windows. A woman comes forward whose curly black hair and alabaster skin look slightly familiar. Names are exchanged, and she says, "Are you Todd's mother?" She went to school with Todd and is a Facebook fan of his.

I meet another nurse who says, "I've been to your house."

"No way," I answer. "When?"

"You had a party to remember the old neighborhood barn when it came down. My husband grew up in your neighborhood."

"You're Richie's wife?"

"I am."

What a small world. I feel right at home. The chemo date is set. Waiting is almost over.

# THE PORT

It is time to have the port put in. I couldn't have anything to eat this morning, so I had a big breakfast at eleven o'clock last night. Varying one's eating schedule is fun, and I highly recommend it. I arrive at the hospital in sort of a balanced state. With a history of *surprises,* I find relaxing a bit difficult. I am ushered into a pre-op room, put on a gown (top clothes off only), and settle down. A nurse tries to find a vein for my IV. He can't find one. I mean, why am I here? He finally finds one, but it is curly and gives him all kinds of trouble with the drip. My confidence level starts to slip.

Then there are questions about what medications I am allergic to, and records have to be accessed. I endure more waiting and more adjusting of the IV, which apparently is up against the wall of the vein. This isn't bad, but it hurts a little. My confidence level slides down another notch.

I get the bright idea to ask the nurse what the port looks like. He gets out samples, and good grief, that sucker is big—a little bigger than a quarter and about one half inch thick. I stare at it, realizing that it will be put *in my body under my skin.* We're talking cutting and inserting here. Then I ask, "What about those two tubes coming out from it?"

"Oh, they go into your jugular vein," answers the nurse. My *what?* At this point, I'm considering escape, but I'm wearing this floppy gown, and how fast can I run in socks? So I remain on the bed. Two younger guys walk into the room wearing bandanas on their heads and khaki scrubs that make them look like inmates. One is heavily tattooed. *You've got to be kidding,* I think. *Please, God,* I pray fervently, *don't make one of them the doctor.*

The two men approach my gurney and wheel me into the hall. On the way, a man brushes past me, grins, and says "Hi. I'm Dr. X, and I'll be putting in your port." *What? Who?* At least he wasn't tattooed. Well, there's no escaping now. I'm stuck. Even if I could take these two guys down and run in my socks, I'd need a GPS to find my way out.

I make it through the procedure, and the tattooed techs, who turn out to be very kind, wheel me back to the pre-op room. Starbucks? You bet.

# I BECOME TOXIC

The topic was chemotherapy. My seatmate on the New Jersey train to Manhattan was adamant. "Chemo is cruel, brutal, and primitive," he said emphatically. I agreed. "I wish there was something less invasive, less devastating," he said, looking out the window. As we neared Newark, he began to gather his things. "I'm flying out to the Southwest to a medical conference," he said rising from his seat. "I was one of the doctors who developed chemotherapy," he continues, looking back at me.

I'd always had negative feelings about chemo. Why would anyone want to take poison? Whenever I was in the neighborhood of our local cancer center, I would look at the building with dread, pitying anyone who had to be inside. When I heard that friends were having chemo, I felt scared, wishing they could have other treatments.

Why, then, am I going to my first treatment in a state of calm and acceptance? I slept like a baby last night and woke refreshed. I am in a private room off the larger infusion room, and I welcome that privacy. Seated in a comfortable lounge chair with a heated blanket that matches my socks and a nurse who is at my beck and call, I feel as if I am in a spa. At one point, I doze, dreaming that I am on the couch at home and David is next to me, his arm around my shoulders. I wake and realize where I am. David is not present. Yet still I feel the gentle pressure of an arm around my shoulders.

I am well-armed with Andrew's teddy, my prayer shawl, and my mobile statue of Mary, who goes everywhere with me in my purse. I visualize the chemo coming into my body as light, sweeping away any rogue cancer cells and allowing my other cells to rise up and bloom. David brings in a delicious lunch, complete with one of the best chocolate cookies I've ever eaten.

I am receiving Cyclophosphamide (Cytoxan) and Taxotere (Docetaxel). The first drug is a treatment for cancer and the second an anti-cancer drug. I am aware of the love and support of my friends and family. I think about *now*, this moment, which is sunny and beautiful.

# CHANGES

When our son Todd was born forty-eight years ago, my mother's friends were aghast that I was having the baby here and not in the nearest city. The hospital was small then, and all three of our children were born there. Now the hospital is not only in a different location but is a sprawl of buildings, including a nursing care home, a state-of-the-art emergency department, and a surgical wing. It has partnered with a larger hospital in a nearby city. There is a helipad next to the emergency department, and the roof is covered with antennae.

There are changes in me. One enters a different space during illness. Because so many external activities have been erased from my present life, I am more aware of the many levels of existence experienced when one is deeply in the moment. I have moved out of the little boxes of routine and thought that I had created.

I am toxic. I am my own version of the Salton Sea. Yesterday afternoon, I had a shot to boost my white cell count, as the chemo I'm taking destroys white blood cells. "You might have pain in your bones and joints because the white cell activity is being ramped up," the nurse informs me. "How do you manage your pain?"

"Manage my pain? I've never had any pain that required managing," I reply. This is another surprise, another thing to learn.

I develop a rash on my face and chest, an allergic reaction to the shot. It is hot but doesn't itch. I'm not feeling well. *Why have I allowed myself to get involved in this treatment? What is going on in my body? What have I done to it?* Then I remember. *I am not my body. The "I" that goes on forever and has been forever, the little part of me that "is" always, will not be touched by these chemicals. This is not happening to me but to the suit I wear while on earth. I can take care of the body. My choice to be treated with allopathic medicine was a choice for my care, a choice to eradicate my cancer.*

I flip through a catalog while waiting for sleep and am stopped by a plaque saying "Courage is more exhilarating than fear, and in the long run it is easier." Eleanor Roosevelt. I have always been blessed to find just the right book or article when I need it.

This morning after breakfast, which did not stay down, I read an article called "Healing Newtown." I read it despite being in tears during the first paragraph. I hold al Fattah, my care bear, and cry all over again. My heart is pierced not only by the killing of the innocent school children but what has happened to the townspeople. They have reached out in so many ways. They have experienced changes in themselves, their newness forged out of fire and tears. My trial is small, but it is enough. I need to be here, in this darkness. It is part of my development. I *will* transcend. This is what healing is all about.

Many years ago, Dave came home from school bent over. "What happened?" I asked, fearing a fall.

"I bent over to pick up a piece of paper and threw my back out. I'm going to bed." I went in to check on him and found him half in and half out of bed, his white face contorted in pain. He appeared to have aged twenty years. All I could think about was, *This is what is meant by "in sickness and health."* When one first hears that phrase while standing at the altar, vibrantly healthy and full of positive expectations, it seems unreal. But then illness strikes. David has risen to the role of my caretaker admirably, a benevolent presence, even communicating without words.

The effects of chemo have been leaping and dancing through my body all weekend. It has been painful, disquieting, and messy. I can't take a shower because of the new port. Suzanne comes to wash my hair while David offers sympathy and cleans up. We have become a maze of medicine. An anti-nausea prescription turned out not to be covered by my insurance and cost $130 out of pocket. Not my pocket.

I watch Gia, who has a serious case of cabin fever. Out she goes; in she comes. She looks wistfully out the window and then skulks around knocking little objects off the shelf, her signal for us to pay attention to her unhappiness. *Soon it will be spring, Gia, and we'll both run around causing all kinds of trouble.* As the comedian Lenny Berman used to say, "Keep your knockers up" (or in my case, knocker).

There is a storm, and needles of ice tattoo the house. Inside, the fire burns brightly, and the storm is held at bay. Gia insists on going out but soon comes in wet and shivery. We wrap her in a towel and dry her, and she settles in her favorite chair and goes to sleep, content. Our homes are our refuge.

When I was a child, each time I saw rays of light shooting down from puffy clouds, I would exclaim, "Look! There's going to be a miracle." My friend's mothers would cluck and say I was the most unusual child they had ever known (which is adult polite for "You're nuts, kid"). I had no doubt that my prediction was correct. Little did I know that the miracle I hoped for was not going to be but was. I was not only looking at the possible miracle but living in one. The sky, the ground, my friends, my body are true miracles.

We get so mixed up with the spill on the floor, the missed appointment, or the medical diagnosis that we forget every breath is a miracle. The Sufis say that the only sin is to forget God for even one second. "Forgive me for forgetting you," I pray but too infrequently.

Today I poke my head out in the twenty-one degree morning and hear a chorus of birdcalls. It's still March, but the grass is a little greener, and the willow trees are turning yellow. I fix a cup of broth, go back to bed, and read, a decadent pleasure.

I am dehydrated. David takes me into the cancer center, where I am put into a wheelchair and wheeled into the infusion room. My oncologist is shocked that I've had so much trouble with the infusion. (You're not alone, honey.) I have an injection of Ringer's solution. I am thankful for that power port. My nurse has wonderful hands. Her touch is warm and confident. She steps in effortlessly and does what needs to be done. I have always had great respect for nurses and the work they do but never more than now. David went for a walk while I was being dripped and saw thousands of geese flying. "It was quite an experience," he tells me on returning. "The sky was black with geese."

Tonight I get up to go to the bathroom and, looking out the window, see three deer in our yard very close to the house. Two are lying down, and the third pushes its nose in the snow, looking for grass. I often wonder what goes on in the silent secrets of the night. Tracks in the snow indicate that we have many visitors then. Indeed, the property is all theirs during that dark mystery.

Gia went out earlier this morning, and now she jumps into the window box, peering anxiously into the house. I open the door, and she pushes in before it is fully open. I don't blame her; it's cold out and snowing—again.

Just now, I noticed sun on a wall that never sees sun because of its location. The sun is being reflected from our car in the driveway. Some places never do get light, and it is our job to reflect what light we are given.

I am learning how to manage being toxic. Here are some rules: always have your water bottle and ChapStick with you, eat small bits of food when you are hungry or feel weird, and listen to your body. Is your stomach gurgling? Are you sleepy or just out of options? There is no schedule for eating or sleeping. Always close the lid before flushing. One must have protected sex. In the care kit given to me by the cancer center, there are several packages of condoms. This made us laugh, as Dave had a vasectomy forty years ago. What's a condom? First David had to stay away from me because I was radioactive. Now it's because I'm toxic. Is there anything in the marriage ceremony about that?

I think of the wonderful healing power of my body and the healing gifts of the universe. Remembering the lifeboat of friends who support me and keep me afloat as I ride a treacherous sea gives me hope.

# HOW WOULD YOU LIKE TO GO TO HOLLYWOOD?

## (OR, THINGS OFTEN AREN'T WHAT THEY SEEM)

When I was a preteen, I dreamed of going to Hollywood. Hollywood was the mecca of all that was glamorous and fun, and I wanted to be there. Most of all, I wanted to see the MGM studios and eat in the commissary with all the actors bustling about in costumes. I did get to Hollywood eventually—not as a starstruck kid but as a mom. Our son Todd lives in Hollywood. His street runs into Sunset Boulevard. When he worked on the TV show *Jeopardy*, we watched a filming of the show. I think *Jeopardy* was filmed in the studio where the old Lucy TV series was shot. Todd gave us a tour of the former MGM lot, and we saw many studios where old favorites were filmed, including the Esther Williams movies.

It's different now. Todd's neighborhood is home to many Russian immigrants. The day care house behind their apartment is for Russian children, and only Russian is spoken there. In other words, Hollywood is home to ordinary people. Glamor is applied and taken off, just that. As a preteen, I would have found this dismaying but not anymore. We do get our wishes in ways we don't expect and when we are ready for them, even if we don't know it.

Today is the day for a milkshake. I can eat whatever I want, and I want a milkshake. When I was a teenager, I loved milkshakes, especially a black and white: a vanilla milkshake with chocolate ice cream. The problem was, few waitresses knew how to make a black and white. I would patiently explain what I wanted and even tell them how to make it. Ordering a black and white got to be an irksome chore. Then one day at lunch, I ordered my usual vanilla milkshake with chocolate ice cream. The waitress didn't say a thing. "At last," I said, breathing a sigh of relief. Soon the waif returned, placing a vanilla milkshake and a dish of chocolate ice cream in front of me.

Not daring to mention a black and white when we go through the drive-in at Wendy's, I accept what they dish out: a smoothie, Wendy's version of a milkshake. I stick in the straw and sip. Nothing happens. I sip again. Still nothing happens. I begin stabbing my straw around and around in the dense liquid. Finally, I get a place near the edge where I can get a satisfying sip. This improves as we drive home, and by the time we get to the end of our ten-minute drive, I'm actually drinking. But I really don't like it that much.

I see the surgeon today, and he smiles, saying, "Even though the wound isn't totally healed, you don't need to wear a bandage on it."

"No more special showers. No more having to poke and clean and cover," I say, looking at Dave. "Yippee!"

"Congratulations," the surgeon replies. "You don't need to come back until June. This is a real milestone for you." His compassion rating skyrockets.

I'm munching on prunes, as I no longer have diarrhea. But guess why I'm munching on prunes.

I walk into the hall bathroom, and the first thing I see is the guest towel rack holding towels covered with pretty little hearts. *Good grief,* I think and pull spring towels out of the linen closet. I find the bunny soap dispatcher, which I place on the sink, even though it doesn't work. Dave brings out the box of Easter decorations, and I hold each fuzzy bunny, chick, and duck to my cheek, welcoming them back. What is it about cute little fuzzy things at Easter? Perhaps it's the idea of renewal, of hope. Or maybe it's just the idea of cute.

The birds are twitter-pated. Two male cardinals went at each other this morning, fighting over territory. The starlings are doing their funny little mating dance. It may be cold out there, but there's plenty going on under the sheets.

# THE GAUZE PADS GO, AND SO DOES THE HAIR

My visiting nurse comes today. With a flourish, I give her a box holding gauze pads, sterile wipes, and tape. My weight has stabilized, and I am eating pretty much what I want. Earlier today, I ran my fingers through my hair and came away with a handful of the stuff. So it begins....

David is at the barbershop having his head shaved in solidarity, which isn't much of a sacrifice, since he doesn't have much to begin with. I can't wait to see what he looks like, especially what he and his barber decide to do with his beard. My hair continues to come out in bits and dribbles. You've heard of silver threads amongst the gold. Here, we have silver threads among just about everything in the house. I see having no hair as a new adventure. Think of it: shower and go, something I've never been able to do. No messing with shampoos, rinses, mousse, hair dryers, and curling irons. If I don't like the hairdo of the day, I can take it off and put on another one, or a scarf and hat, or a *turban.*

There are catalogues full of hats, and I'm licking my chops. I have three darling hats that I've worn already. I like them so much I think I will wear them AC (after chemo). Of course, I also have some gigantic earrings.

When I was a little girl, I used to love to play dress up. My mother called me Mrs. Picklepuss. Well, now I get to be Mrs. Picklepuss all over again, dressing up and having a grand old time.

Dave looks fantastic. What is it about being bald that makes men look sexy? He is sporting a goatee, which enhances his handsome face. I'm still losing hair. "It's like living with a Russian wolfhound who is shedding," he complains while sweeping up. I ball up a bunch of fallen hair and put it outside, hoping the birds will use it for nesting material. Heaven knows it's soft. My scalp hurts, another surprise.

Dave and I go for a walk in a land that is dead and gray. It's not the same as November, when things are settling down, preparing for sleep. Deep reds, greens, and gold paint the November landscape. March is simply the debris of winter. For this month to make sense, one has to get close to the ground, for that is where things are happening. One has to listen, especially in the morning. Todd describes March best. Only when one has gone through the long, dark tunnel of an upstate New York winter can one truly experience spring.

Today is Good Friday, the day Christians commemorate Jesus' suffering on the cross, a good time to consider what suffering means. The etymology of the word, according to Helen Luke in her book *Old Age,* is from the Latin verb *ferre,* which means "to bear, to carry." With the prefix *sub,* meaning under, this reminds us of "undercarriage," that which bears the weight of the carriage above the wheels. This, then, is uplifting, not weight bearing down. We have been culturally led to believe that the antidote to suffering is to feel happy, to fill one's mind with glad thoughts. Not so. One has to plunge into the heart of suffering, not to draw away or go around it. The only way out of suffering is to go through it. In doing this, one experiences a new meaning, a different level of being. With that awareness comes the inner knowing that through this experience, the weight and suffering of mankind is carried, the darkness of the world's miseries lifted in some small degree. While I accept this theory, I have not yet lived it: perhaps not until now.

Hair day! My friend Zaynab told me she would shave her head in solidarity. When I informed Suzanne of this, she said, "I will, too, if Paul doesn't object. It's taken me five years to get it this long," she adds wistfully, leading me to believe that she won't cut it. But Paul thinks it would be a great idea, so here we are at my hair salon after hours: Suzanne, Zaynab, her husband Wadud, Dave, and me. Our little party takes up the entire studio. My beautician doesn't like the idea of bald. "I'll clip your hair very short so you can be supportive and still look good," she says with a jaunty smile, her trademark. First she tackles Suzanne's hair, which falls off in brown chunks. *I never liked that color,* I think, surveying the floor. The style she has created is darling, perfect for Suzanne, who smiles as she tosses her head.

Next comes Zaynab, and as her cut hair cascades to the floor, years fall off as well. My process is different. Clippers buzz my hair. All I can think of is a picture from the annals of World War II showing women being marched through the streets of some war-torn city, their hands behind bald heads. The crime, if I remember correctly, was collaborating with the Nazis.

So in my baldness, I join the sisterhood of chemo recipients and Nazi collaborators, all of us victims if we choose to be. My cropped head is washed, and it feels as if she is washing hair. Perhaps it is a sensation similar to the phantom limb of an amputee.

It is 8:15 when we leave the salon. I am wearing my new wig. It feels scratchy. Will it fall off? I reach up and pat my head. Then I do it all over again. We're having too much fun to go home, so we go to a restaurant for a late dinner. The place is packed. Will I see anyone I know? We wait and wait for a table. This is the first time I've been to a restaurant in over six weeks, and I'm enjoying every minute. Zaynab reaches out and takes my hand. "We need to turn our unfortunate times into parties," she says. This evening wasn't just about cutting hair. It was about love.

# THE EASTER SEASON IS UPON US

I had surmised, this being Easter, my thoughts would be about resurrection. However, when I woke around five o'clock a.m., I was angry. This was the first real anger I have felt since my diagnosis. Today is the first Easter we haven't been with our grandsons in ten years. I think of our friends who are traveling or are in their winter quarters, and my anger grows. *I'm going to miss spring,* I wail inwardly. I feel as if I were a car parked beside the road, watching traffic flow past me.

Yet I know I am lucky. My cancer is gone. The treatments are so it won't sneak under the radar and come back. I have a kind, loving caretaker and friends who support me in many ways. I get to see our daughter Suzanne often during the week. Get well cards and flowers are now staples in our house. How can I possibly be angry?

In being angry, I am living both in the past and in the future. I concentrate on the now, that tiny point that encapsulates all time. My anger dissolves. We are resurrected with every breath we take, constantly evolving. This wisdom is my Easter gift.

Looking out the window, I see a small parade of people headed toward the house across the street. It is the parade of centuries, the parade of family coming to celebrate a holiday. A month ago, our neighbor Eve stopped me at our mailbox, which is next to hers. "Kurt has pancreatic cancer," she stated simply. I didn't know what to say. "He's having chemo now," she continued.

This gave me an opening. "Is he being treated here?"

"Yes, he is."

"Oh, then we can be cancer buddies," I replied stupidly, not wanting to say or even think the obvious. Pancreatic cancer is often fatal. *But it won't be fatal for Kurt. He's too alive, too healthy. Not Kurt.*

This celebration across the road is not just for Easter. It's for Kurt.

This morning, I wake to the sound of the snowplow. The ratchet sound is as tied to winter as are snow and cold. We hear it as the plow scrapes its way along the road. When we were working, the sound signified snowy or icy roads, and we groaned inwardly. Since we've retired, we just snuggle down and pull the covers tighter. But this morning, we don't want snow. It's April, for heaven's sake. Looking out the window, I see a snow-covered ground. It looks ridiculous and out of place. The trees stand as proud sentinels, bare and black, frowning at the weather. As do we. As do we.

On the first Tuesday of every month, we host a small group meeting that includes a shared meal, some teaching about a book we are currently reading, and a discussion. We are responsible for the main dish, and others bring side dishes, creating a feast.

On this night, people arrive, arms laden with flowers, goodies, and extra delights. Eileen volunteered to provide the main dish, as cooking is out of the question for me. Lola comes in, a broad smile on her face, arms laden with food, her signature cup of Starbucks and a purple gift bag. "Open it," she says, thrusting it at me, "right now." I open it and stare into a huge nest of Cadbury cream eggs.

"I've never seen so many," I exclaim.

"When I was last here, you told me there had been no Easter candy in your house this year and that you'd missed eating Cadbury cream eggs. Well, here they are," she finishes with a flourish.

Lola had made the egg search into a mission, going store to store *after the Easter egg sales* and buying what eggs were left in stock. She'd found fifty-seven, and they were all in the gift bag. "Enough to get you through the rest of your treatments," she says as she moves further into the house, her long skirts swishing.

As people prepare to go home, I stand at the door speechless, wondering how on earth I can adequately thank everyone. As I stammer, Zaynab comes to my rescue. "This is what love looks like," she says simply.

# THE SECOND INFUSION

Suzanne accompanies me to the cancer center, and Eddie's teddy bear comes along this time. I take the laughing pig, a toy pig that rolls on the floor emitting deep belly laughs. It's impossible to watch him and not at least giggle, and soon everyone in the infusion room is howling with laughter. My doctor had promised to lower the dosage but changes his mind at the last minute. "Hey, do you remember how sick I was last time?" I ask hopefully.

"Oh. No, I forgot. I'm sorry." I can tell by the expression on his face that he truly is sorry. He's always telling me I look and act sixty-five years old, which is flattering. But really I am seventy-five, and my body is ten years older than he thinks it is. We'll see what happens.

I force my mind away from thinking toxic during the process, which is taking forever. Again I visualize the chemicals as white light coursing through my body, aggressively seeking out rogue cells and killing them. I think of my other cells as spring cells waiting to come back to life.

I have so many papers from my insurance company that I create a new notebook. They have been wonderful through this illness. Not so my prescription carrier. This morning, we discovered that my prescription insurance company is refusing to recognize me under any name. The pharmacy has fed all my names into the computer. It's the name thing again.

I've had the injection that will rev up my white cell manufacturing centers. While we wait for yet another prescription to be filled, we drive to Abbott's to welcome spring with their famous frozen custard. I'm beginning to feel at home with no hair, and I've sort of accepted the way I look. Our world hasn't turned completely upside down, but it's different, a place where we see and feel things differently, more deeply.

The next morning, the first thing I see upon awakening is an arsenal of pill bottles on my bedside table. *Ugh*, I think, *sick person.* Then I remember that these little pills are supposed to keep me from tossing my cookies all weekend, so I regard them with kindness. I have enough anti-nausea pills to open a pharmacy.

Remembering that Kyle is coming from Moyersville today, I happily get out of bed. He arrives around midmorning. I pep up just at the sight of his handsome face. He is tall, six foot one, and at forty-six has a full head of gray hair, making a nice contrast to his dark eyes. We sit in the living room sipping fruit drinks. The sun shines in the window, bringing out the rich, dark tones of the room. Later, Suzanne and Paul join us for dinner, which, thanks to the pills, I can eat. We laugh, reliving childhood memories. I watch, framing this scene, these precious moments.

It is morning, and there are delightful activities going on around me. Dave is making blueberry pancakes while Kyle brews coffee. We have a three-cup-of-coffee breakfast, long and loving. Now the neighborhood is alive with sounds of early spring. Kyle drives the mower and attached wagon around the yard picking up sticks and branches. He and David have taken down the snow fence. Our neighbors till the soil in their vegetable gardens and prune grapevines. The tulips need to be sprayed so they won't be eaten by deer. The Christmas rose is in full bloom, a gorgeous pink. Kyle takes off his jacket and continues working in his tee shirt. It must be warm out there. I am the quiet observer. Like Cliff Bradshaw, I am a camera, a recorder of sound and image.

# SLOWLY THE DAYS GO BY

It has been raining, making the grass greener. I hope the deer are eating grass and not my budding flowers. This morning, there are droplets of ice on the branches. I can see ice on the trees in the woods, so I hope the temperature goes up, preventing ice from accumulating. My visiting nurse came today and said she was checking me for collateral damage. This is a good phrase. I don't even want to think about what is happening to my body. I feel as if my insides have turned to tin. I can taste it in my mouth.

I dip into my box of positive thoughts and come up empty. As a result of the infusion, I have rosy cheeks, something new on my usually pale face. My friend Patrice tells me I look sun-kissed, but even that observation doesn't cheer me. I am at a low, low point. Not sure if I am even curing, I reject the idea of healing. It's just bunk and doesn't work.

There is fog outside. I open the door to let Gia out and hear an opera of birdcalls coming from the mist. If I hurry, perhaps I can find Brigadoon. But the fog lifts quickly, leaving a curtain of white that floats above the fields like a wraith. Then the rains come. I settle in a chair and read.

I still have vivid pink cheeks, and with a scarf on, I look like a jolly Russian peasant woman, which is a step up from a Nazi collaborator. I have itchy, peeling hands. My visiting nurse told me to try bag balm. Back in the days when bag balm was just for cows, I used to run over to the neighborhood barn for the salve when the traveling farm supply truck showed up. This was for my own little calf, Suzanne, who had terminal diaper rash.

Despite all the pills, I'm still vomiting. But I have found my focus once again. Losing that was the worst part of chemo hell. I carry on, continuing to learn. I can now pronounce prochlorperazine. This may not seem like much of a big deal, but for one who is phonetically challenged, it is a major breakthrough. The itch in my hands is now everywhere. Fortunately, only one area at a time is affected. It should be interesting if all this skin peels.

The last time I looked at our garden, only a few green things were showing. Now it is filled with green leaves, and the daffodils are in bud. We can't stop spring from coming. This is true grace.

I need to go back to the cancer center for another IV. While I am being dripped, Dave buys a hot dog and goes down to the lakefront to eat it. He enjoys watching people fishing, walking, and setting out picnics. As soon as the weather gets better, we upstate New Yorkers are ready to roll.

Not me, however. I think I'm good for a walk to the mailbox, but I will be clinging to my hero who gets me there and back.

# NIGHTTIME, FLOWERS, AND PRETZELS

I have become in sync with the secrets of the night. Usually, I stay in the warm comfort of my bed, a place of security. This is my nighttime castle, the place where I am whisked away to dreams. To step out of this womb would be to enter another world: one of cold and dark. To open the bedroom door would be to leave all nighttime security and be buffeted about by whatever is on the other side, surely not the familiar hallway. But tossing and turning are doing me no good and certainly not helping Dave's sleep, so I rise and slip through the darkness, out the door. Even with the light on, the hall looks different, as if transposed into a more subtle reality. Gia performs a perfect yoga stretch and then settles back on her haunches to regard me. This is not her usual routine. *Should I eat or go outdoors*? she seems to ponder. Disregarding either option, she disappears into the dark recesses of the house. I wrap up in my special blanket and settle on the couch. There is utter silence. All the humans on the road are asleep, cars parked, lawnmowers silent. Only the animals are awake, and they roam carefully out of doors, out of sight. Everything is black outside my little circle of light. But this isn't as bad as I thought. I get more used to the night house, its creaks and sighs, and begin to read my book, trying to hide from insomnia in the cold horrors of the siege of Leningrad, not the happiest of escapes. Only one car goes down the road, perhaps the paper delivery, until the school bus rattles by, its yellow an early sunrise. I must doze, for when I open my eyes, the dark has disappeared—and with its going, familiarity returns. It's time to get up. When I go into the bedroom, I see that my place on the bed is being protected by Gia, who sneaked through the door I hadn't completely latched.

Pink, apricot, chartreuse, deep green, all blend into a happy arrangement of flowers sitting on the dining room table. I love flowers. Seeing flowers wherever one looks is my idea of the perfect environment. Now I'm looking at daffodils and narcissus surrounding delicate violet and white blooms. For a time, there was a wild arrangement of tulips on the kitchen counter that shone in the afternoon sun, a spectacle I showed up for every day. In the winter, there were spring hothouse flowers that smiled hopefully. From the kitchen, I see lilac bushes leafing out. In my prechemo life, I would have *noticed* the flowers, but I would not have *seen* them. Now I immerse myself in lacy insides, delicate curve of stem.

I'm munching on pretzels, one of three foods I can tolerate. The other two are good cheddar cheese and gingersnaps.

# THE BOSTON BOMBINGS

When I first heard of the Boston bombings, I thought this could not happen to runners who need their legs. But it did. I'm in a position to identify with one's world tipping crazily and turning upside down. One enters another reality, and the identity one once had changes. The unthinkable becomes the norm. Darkness, the sweating grip of pain, or retching sickness may lead one to the breathless gasp, "I can't do this anymore." But at one point, there is a turn, and one heads up, out, forward. One moves away from the tightening grip of defeat. Just as the helpers after the blast ran *toward* the injured, not away, this refusal to collapse speaks to me of overcoming. This is human triumph. This is the triumph of Boston.

I am experiencing chemo skin. Yesterday, my feet itched so badly I dumped cornstarch into my socks. This helped the itching, although my feet left little white footprints all over the house. When I get ready for bed, I rub cornstarch into my arms, shoulders, and chest. Then I rub bag balm on my feet and put on socks. Next I rub bag balm over my hands and put on gloves. Sexy!

I run screaming to my Mary Kay lady for help with my facial skin. She responds with the basics. Mary Kay cosmetics were developed from a formula that was used to soften leather, so take that, chemo skin.

I am reading the White House Chef mystery series, which includes recipes. The one I just finished, *Eggsecutive Orders,* led me to make a fried egg sandwich for lunch. Talk about comfort food. The best thing about a fried egg sandwich is the yolk, which explodes when bitten into, sending gold everywhere in one's mouth before settling into a sunny pool of deliciousness.

# LESSONS

There are three aspects to healing: physical, emotional/ psychological, and spiritual. The physical has to do with managing one's care and listening to the body. When should you rest? Was that the right thing to eat? How much liquid are you consuming?

The emotional/psychological has to do with one's outlook, seeing oneself as well and filled with light, carrying on instead of giving up. This is more difficult than the physical stage, where one mostly follows orders.

The third stage, spiritual, is the most difficult. This is the place where one asks, "What do you have to teach me?" This is where one gets to work. There are no directions here, no map. The answers one seeks are not definitive and may never be revealed. The way is hazy and often dark. But this is perhaps the most important stage of the journey, and what light one has shines into the darkness. It is a small light but steady. It is called hope. It is called faith. It is called healing.

Yesterday, I was looking at a photograph of a friend's son kissing his newborn baby, and I lost it, as they say. But I really hadn't lost anything. I found my heart had been pierced with beauty and love. Chemo has not only has stripped me of health, but it has also uncovered layers from my heart, leaving it open, vulnerable, and able to receive grace. In finding my tears, I've found a connection to the divine.

There are many forms of prayer. One prays in gratefulness or thanksgiving, forgiveness, supplication, and recognition of divine glory. There are prayers that explode from us unbidden as we glimpse the corals and purples of a glorious sunset or look into the eyes of a newborn.

There is another prayer that I've discovered. I call it the last prayer. I came across it out of my own feeling of helplessness and despair the other night. It goes something like this: "Help!" In calling for help, I recognized that I could not heal myself or force my medication toward a quicker cure. My defenses were knocked out, and a channel opened for the divine to step in and do its work. I know from my own experiences and from extensive reading that we are always cared for. I've grown up with the saying "Let go and let God." That never worked for me. I always held on, never entirely releasing my hold. So I cry out for help over and over until my call becomes a mantra.

The next day is filled with many tiny blessings, and I am given the grace to see them. One day, many years ago, a voice came to me asking, "Can you give up everything and follow me?" I answered yes but immediately wanted to take it back. I wasn't exactly sure what giving up entailed. Should I give up my family, friends, house, or job? Who exactly was I to follow?

Now, years later, I am seeing the slow process of that promise. The giving up is internal and has been a slow and often painful process that continues, even giving up and calling for help. I am grateful for each step.

# THE THIRD INFUSION

My oncologist is going to stop chemo after four treatments. I had the third yesterday. The light at the end of the tunnel glows brighter.

The area around the old watering hole on our property is alive with daffodils. Walking through that yellow field, I am reminded of Wordsworth's poem:

> I wandered lonely as a cloud
> That floats on high o'er vales and hills,
> When all at once I saw a crowd,
> A host of golden daffodils;
> Beside the lake, beneath the trees,
> Fluttering and dancing in the breeze...

Our daffodils are a blaze of color, a burst of extravagance. I can pick all I want without guilt, and I do, carrying a bunch home and feeling giddy with excess. Now they spill out of a vase on the kitchen counter, a bright pool of sunshine.

Spring comes to upstate New York like a symphony. The conductor taps his baton, and grass begins to green; willows turn a yellowish tan. Then one by one, other flowers tune in: daffodils, forsythia, hyacinths. Yellow flowers appear first, as if creating extra sunshine to help the others along. Now the bushes and trees begin to leaf out, and tulips and creeping phlox add to the swelling notes of the symphony. New flowers bring the music to its full height in midsummer. Then the notes slow and fade, trailing off to a solo of falling leaves in November.

We would be overwhelmed if everything suddenly bloomed at once. So it is with our awakening. Each new blossom adds to our understanding bit by bit as we build our own gardens, each in its own time, each as we are ready.

With every infusion, the level of chemicals in my body builds. Now I move slowly, painfully, from bed to couch each morning. I am too weak to lift my head and unable to talk, since my voice seems to have abandoned me. The minutes and hours pass slowly, somehow just out of reach. The day slithers between my fingers as I watch helplessly. Chemo, the killing machine, courses through my body attacking everything, almost, but not quite my will to live.

I go to the oncologist twice for fluid, as I can't eat or drink anything. Today I stay in bed all day. Dave comes in with his laptop, and the cat sleeps on the bed.

Time loses its meaning in this veil of illness. It is not a passage of minutes and hours but of light. The intense morning sun comes through our eastern windows, striking the mobile line of mirrors hung just outside, sending reflected brilliance to dance in crazy circles around the room like fairies at a party. Midday sun stays outside, a scene of tranquility. Afternoon sun lights up the kitchen with cheeriness and then scuttles to different parts of the room: the arm of a chair, the red afghan, and a spot on the floor. Late day brings a softening of light, a visible hush. Evening is the time of day when Christ walks the earth in sandaled feet: deep peace, a breath drawn in slowly.

I wonder. Do we pass through time, or does time pass through us?

# MARRIAGE

"Well, you know," I say to Suzanne, "Your father will only take care of the cellar when he is ready to do so. He's like that with a lot of things."

"And you don't say anything?" she asks incredulously.

"Yep," I answer. "It took me fifty-three years to learn that."

Dave and I celebrate our fifty-third wedding anniversary this coming summer. Our marriage has suffered disconnects and occasional near-disasters. Our most challenging time was retirement, when suddenly there was nothing between us but us. For me, it meant seeing the man I had lived with for many years in an entirely new light. Had he always brushed his teeth this way?

But we survived and now have come to what I would call one of the most difficult challenges of our marriage: chemo. This experience has brought us closer than ever.

Now with so many changes in the twilight zone of illness, we have begun to communicate on deeper levels. We don't talk much, but we touch more often. David has been the most patient of caretakers, never once losing his temper or seeming to be disturbed by my many requests. We wondered what it would be like to grow old together. We had high hopes, but never could we have imagined this magic.

Thursdays had been predictable days for us: yoga at seven a.m., breakfast at our favorite place, shopping, and running errands. Not anymore. David goes to yoga, breakfast, and shopping alone. I miss the smell of yoga mats and the good feeling that comes from working the body. I miss talking with friends and especially our breakfast of good home-cooked food topped off with coffee. I miss our favorite waitress, who always has coffee ready for us and keeps a Bible by her cash register.

I miss the hustle and bustle of the supermarket, the wild array of veggies and fruits, lure of baked goods, the solid feel of rows of meat, fish, and poultry. I miss the riotous color of the flower department. Mostly, I miss the people, all shapes and sizes, coming from different places.

I miss the egg farm with its constant beef cattle and perky little beagle. I miss riding down Main Street, checking out the shops as we glide by. I miss the library and its myriad choices, the excitement of a new audiobook. Oddly, I miss the routine.

Today my angel statue arrives under a dark and threatening sky. David is upset because he can't mow the lawn. I understand his frustration but love to watch rain sweep over the fields, green woods a perfect backdrop. But the misty weather soon clears, and the sun peeps through, ready to greet my angel.

Looking at the new garden configuration in the side yard, I realized it needed a focal point. An angel statue would be perfect. Luckily, I found one on the Internet that was for sale. She has just come and awaits installation. "What do you think?" David asks after she is upright.

"Oh, I just love her," I coo, admiring her graceful Grecian pose. The packaging informs us that the angel's name is Patience. "This is perfect," I tell Dave.

"Quite relevant," he laughs, putting his arm around my shoulders.

# THE LAST INFUSION

Thinking ahead to what's coming, I have an emotional meltdown. I don't see how I can go through with it. I visualize myself kneeling at the doctor's feet, pleading with him to stop all medication now. *I will feel better eventually,* I tell myself. But it doesn't work.

"Come on, Mom," Suzanne prompts, hoping to make me feel better. "Let's put the statues out in the garden." We move around the yard placing Saint Francis, Mary, a bevy of baby angels, and fairies among the plants. I'm happy to see my old friends. I feel a little better now.

I get to the infusion center and find everyone ready with new medication (the big guns) and a plan that will hopefully keep me from tossing my cookies. I am cautiously optimistic. Patrice accompanies me, and we have a lovely chat. Both of us agree that from now on, our chats will occur somewhere else over tea.

When I get home, I see Patience and repeat the name to myself over and over. I am flooded with happiness. Perhaps steroids, part of the infusion, are responsible for my euphoria. I think of summer, good things, and new life. All these are there, waiting. I reach for them...

I am a chemo brain on steroids. My mind is going fifty miles an hour (my body about ten). I get an idea and dash into my office; then I stand there wondering what it was I dashed in for. I'll begin a task and then go off and do something else. When I finally do return, I'll look at the mess in front of me and wonder how it got there. I sealed a graduation card without putting in the check. Are these regular signs of aging? Perhaps, but now I have an excuse.

I return to the slow, steady pace that comes after chemo treatment. Time doesn't seem to exist. I sit in my green chair in the living room as the day stretches on. I think of many of our friends who are in different places doing exciting things. I am missing the final training of Healing Circle work. Dave goes out to water and fertilize. A crew spreads mulch in the neighbor's garden. Their boat is in the driveway waiting to be put into the lake. Life is happening in many places, in many forms.

But my life now is this lovely room with its quiet serenity. Gia jumps up on my lap and settles into the soft blanket covering my legs and feet. I observe the shiny blackness of her coat. She wiggles around looking for the most comfortable spot, purring. I pet her gently under her chin, and she raises her head. Do cats smile? She turns and stretches out. I stroke her back gently. We both begin to doze.

I need to be hydrated. I refuse to be dragged to the cancer center yet again. But I must drink. David becomes my coach, encouraging me to drink. Anything in a glass tastes like a melted tin can. I resist. He urges. I angrily resist. He insists. This is not the role either of us was meant to play. David is at the end of his rope, and I have murder on my mind. It's been a brutal week.

As my visiting nurse leaves, she says, "Chemo is a hideous process. You have to be a lion to get through it."

That comment turns everything around. I now know I will make it through. I can't give up the challenge to be a lion.

*Rose in a Storm,* a novel by Jon Katz, is told from the point of view of a farm dog. Reading it brings waves of nostalgia, which in my vulnerable state I indulge. During our early years in this place, life in the neighbor's barn determined the rhythm of our days. Before we were out of bed, the farmer was in the barn, milking cows. Country music blared from an old radio set precariously on a low beam. Clanking milk machines and the stamping of cows' hoofs all blended with the music. Our then-small yard was surrounded on two sides by cows pulling and chewing grass, the sound becoming a lullaby that put us to sleep. Silage was often spread on the ground just beyond our kitchen window, and the cows, a cafeteria of munchers, eyed me benignly as I watched them.

In retrospect, those days seem to be simpler and slower. Cats roamed the barn, and mice and rats scuttled between hay bales, teasing them. Children invented daring games, sailing down ropes and leaping into stored hay. Scruffy farm dogs herded the cows down our dusty dirt road.

Cows and barn are long gone, and the children, now grown, are scattered across the country from coast to coast. Our road is paved, our property now includes the old pasture, and the silage feed is a flower garden. No longer country, we have become a respectable rural suburb with houses spaced between wide lawns. I miss the old days.

Even so, we are lucky to be here. I sigh, reflecting on the morning news of a stabbing that took place in my childhood city neighborhood, just a block from where we lived. I visualize the busy streets and close houses, comparing that scene with the beautiful serenity here, where we have lived for over fifty years. *I escaped,* I think gratefully. But what of those who could not get out?

# THE NEXT STEP: RADIATION

## INTERMISSION

The radiologist is immediately likeable. He has the round and happy face of a benevolent grandfather. Moreover, he seems to have the gift of being able to relate to a patient's feelings.

"I'm scheduling another CAT scan because of the heavy lymph node involvement of your cancer. I want to make sure everything is clear before we begin radiation."

"And if it's not?" I query.

"If anything is found, more chemotherapy will be needed."

*No!* I want to scream. *Not again. Please, not again.*

My insides crawl with fear as I sit quietly listening to him tell about the side effects of radiation, remembering that all my cancer survivor friends tell me that this process is no big deal. The treatment won't start until June and will go on daily for five weeks. I try to focus on my upcoming vacation from all medical procedures.

David and Suzanne have gone to the Adirondacks for Ann's memorial service. I am sad that I'm not well enough to attend, but I'm used to missing events. *Being alone has a sanctity all its own,* I muse as silence settles around me. It's warm in the evening, so I throw open windows that have been sealed shut for some time. A chant of birdsong drifts in on a welcome breeze. The birds are saying good night to one another. After they are quiet, crickets will take up the chorus, their soothing songs a blanket of sound covering the dark night.

Today is my maiden voyage into the real world. Friend Eileen spent the night and suggests we go out to breakfast. I am bubbleheaded as we enter the restaurant. I am wearing a turban, which I hope looks stylish and not as if it's covering a chemo head. I look around the familiar restaurant, taking in its rustic décor and the framed Groucho Marx quote: "Outside of a dog, a book is man's best friend. Inside of a dog, it's too dark to read." I know the bathroom walls are lined with photos of customers and their dogs.

"Eileen," I whisper in disbelief. "I can't drink the coffee. It tastes terrible."

"You're kidding," she responds, using her signature phrase. "Mine's delicious."

"It's not the coffee, it's my taste buds." I pick at what is usually my favorite breakfast choice, lox and bagels, managing to eat just enough not to embarrass myself.

Exhausted, I spend the rest of the day in front of the TV. It was worth it. I'm coming back.

I'm picking through an exciting display of summer sandals in the hospital gift shop, which is conveniently located next to the imaging department. This is my reward for drinking a big bottle of liquid, being injected with a dye that makes me feel as if I'm going to pee, and being wheeled in and out of yet another giant machine. I examine jeweled flip-flop sandals in red, yellow, and white and leave with two pair, feeling entitled.

The CAT scan is clear, so with a sigh of relief, I continue on the long road to recovery. The literature says that when one finishes chemotherapy, it doesn't mean one is back to normal. All I need to do is think of my black fingernails, peeling skin on my feet, the strange feeling of neuropathy in my hands and feet, cellulitis on my ankle, and bald head to realize the job that chemo has done on my body.

I bury myself in the color and vibrancy of flowers in our yard. The rhododendrons are firecrackers of pink blossoms. Like tiny trumpets, their stamens are a visible music. The three outward petals on the iris have a fuzzy base like a tiny caterpillar, while the other three fold in gracefully. This reminds me of a balanced life that honors both inner and outer. Only the hand of the divine could fashion such intricate yet functional loveliness.

My visiting nurses have signed off my case. These are the ladies who put me on house arrest and made me take up all the throw rugs in the house so I wouldn't fall. While each nurse has a unique and interesting personality, auburn-haired Helen was the one who came most often and therefore the one I know best. Above and beyond the call of duty, she once took me for a walk, watered my parched garden, and bought cookies for me. She sits easily on the floor, preferring this to a chair. Helen knows a great deal about anything medical and watches over me like a hawk. Nothing escapes her attention. I expect a prolonged farewell, even hugs, as she prepares to leave. She says goodbye and opens the door, and a strange gap of silence stretches between us, making her parting more professional than personal. Then she is gone.

I ponder the many partings in my life. What and whom will I remember from this phase of the journey? My plan has been to shred all medical notes while drinking champagne. I will blot out 2013 altogether. But I wonder what memories will creep through my carefully constructed walls. What faces will appear in my mind, what voices will speak?

I turn off the TV and welcome the sudden quiet. Without the shrill of television voices, I notice the rain outside. I am a lover of the intimacy of rain. Clouds of steam rise from the woods, and the lake is blotted from view. Tree limbs bow down, birds fly for cover, and the world is most privately here, just here. Gia comes in from her outdoor adventures and curls up to sleep, having nothing better to do. Sound is concentrated on the drops of water hitting the leaves, rain swooshing through the gutters. Time seems to stand still, a breath drawn in slowly. I stay in this moment deeply, not considering past or future.

# MEET THE KIDS

As I walk through the maze of halls at the hospital led by three young techs who do not wear bandanas, I think about all that has been done to my body. Now I am to be marked. The techs are from the radiation department, and the marks will help direct the lineup of the machine.

Suddenly, I realize that I know where I am. Signs around me point to ultrasound, MRI, and CAT scan, my destination. I can escape through those double doors at the end of the corridor, but I won't. After being hospital gowned, I get on the table and swim in and out of the machine, which clicks and murmurs like a benevolent nanny. After pictures are taken, including snapshots, the marking ceremony begins. I am being tattooed. Suzanne and I had vowed to get tattoos when I turned seventy, but we never went through with it. I now know we never will, because this hurts. Why do people volunteer to have ink put beneath their skin with a needle? I am duly marked with my own private black dots: forever.

The techs lead me back to the cancer center, which is connected to the hospital. We talk about the question of the day, a riddle or question that is posted daily in the radiology unit. Today's question is "What TV program were Dick and Harry on?"

I have no clue. "Well, you really have to go way back. This show was on a long time ago," one tech tells me.

"Oh, when was it on?" I ask, expecting to hear the fifties or sixties.

"In the late nineties."

"The late nineties? That was only a few minutes ago," I exclaim.

The techs say nothing.

When one is over sixty-five, all medical personnel are usually not only younger but more knowledgeable. I sigh, feeling like the ancient mariner.

# HAIR WISPS

I see a few baby wisps of hair. Will it all come back? What color will it be? Will I have curls, or will it be straight? Through color changes and permanents, I have learned not to mess with what God gave me: pewter-gray, straight-as-string hair.

Being bald definitely has its advantages. Taking a shower is a piece of cake. Turn off the water, run a towel over your head, and you're done. No shampooing. No conditioner. No hair dryer. No cowering in the rain or wind, fearing flat hair. No such thing as a bad hair day.

I'll just wait and see what happens. Stay with the process. Trust the divine. Be creative with what *is*.

# THE WORLD BECKONS

The creek is raging, water level with the banks. We later learn that creek had flooded, carrying away a gazebo. We cross a bridge and step onto ground oozy beneath the grass. This is my first big venture out. Can I make it to the yurt where the workshop honoring our earth is being held? This is the longest walk I have undertaken. I get there. Later, as part of the program, we are led to a glade near the creek. It is like entering a womb of green. Here we do breathing exercises, honoring the elements: earth, air, fire, and water. I breathe in and out for each element. Even the rain that only days before had caused the creek to be destructive seems to be a blessing. Water rushes by now, creating an energy that fills the glen, entering our bodies. Movements are added to our breathing, and I begin to flow in this slow dance beside the pounding water. As I move, I feel a subtle difference in my body. Something begins happening to me. During my worst times, I abandoned the idea of healing, even thinking of it as a silly superstition. Yet I now feel this change, this sense of renewal. Much later, I am to realize that my healing began here.

# ANOTHER SURGERY

Taking advantage of the gap between treatments, I have much-needed cataract surgery performed. This time, I arrive at the surgical department at 10:30 a.m. I expect the receptionist to say, "Oh, good morning, Mrs. Johnson. How nice to see you again. Would you like your usual gurney?" The place is full, the prep room slots all taken. I must wait for a volunteer to put new sheets on my little bed. Once again, I sign away my life after reading about the terrible things that could happen to me, ending with death, which comes after brain damage. This is airport surgery; flights stacked awaiting descent, arrivals every other minute. I am examined, whisked into surgery, and in no time I'm out and ready to go home, this time with a new eye.

# A SHIFT IN PATIENTS

Being the caretaker is my new role. All attention now shifts to David, who has just spent four days in the hospital. His problem, as it turns out, is acid reflux. A symptom of this condition can be pains in the chest, which is what caused all the concern because Dave has some heart issues.

Privately, Suzanne and I wonder if Dave's difficulty could be caretaker's dilemma. He has cared day and night for me these many months, and that could have an effect on his health and well-being. While he is hospitalized, Suzanne and I slip out to a restaurant for lunch. Later I hear via the grapevine that someone saw me and asked, "What happened to Jacqueline? She looks awful."

Oh, dear.

# I *DO* HAVE LYMPHEDEMA

During my check-up appointment with the surgeon, I reread the postings on his door. Each has a different meaning than it did at the beginning of my procedures. One of them especially resonates. "Giving and receiving is the same thing." After months of being unable to do much for myself, I have developed a backlog of guilt. I've been struggling with receiving help graciously. This gives me hope.

I have lymphedema. When my surgeon told me that this might be a possible outcome of my mastectomy, I was horrified. Now that it is a reality, I am devastated. I will not only have to wear a compression sleeve but a glove as well. I can cover a sleeve but not a glove. I don't want this ugly thing on my arm and hand. For the first time since the cancer diagnosis, I feel as if my body has betrayed me.

But happily, I am driving again. With my new eye and glasses, I can see well enough to get behind the wheel, a safe driver. I opt to drive a short distance for my maiden voyage, with David riding shotgun. The car feels very big, and I'm not sure I can put it in all the right places. This will take practice.

I have my new compression sleeve. The flesh color blends in better than I'd thought, and it feels like having a built-in massage. Yes, it's ugly. Having to rinse it out every night is a pain. Now when I see someone wearing a medical device, I react with empathy rather than dread. Being ill brings with it new depths of compassion for others.

Being ill has also given me a deeper appreciation of nature. While house arrest is over, I am still pretty much confined to our 4.6 acres. Wandering the yard, I talk to the flowers, telling them how gorgeous they are. I truly think they respond by puffing up with pride. I read once that we should embrace the morning. I breathe deeply, embracing the morning, the afternoon, embracing summer. I take in the early sunlight and mentally dance in the long shadows of shade, learning from what the mystic Hazrat Inayat Kahn calls "the one holy book, the sacred manuscript of nature, the only scripture that can enlighten the reader."

Zen master Jingcen of Changsha was once asked, "How do you turn the mountains, rivers, and great earth and return to the self?"

He replied, "How do you turn the self and return to the mountains, rivers, and great earth?"

# I AM RADIATED

The radiation treatments have begun. Every day at 2:45 p.m., I appear at the radiation department in the cancer center, put on a hospital gown, and check the daily riddle written on a white board in the waiting room. "Name ten parts of the body that only have three letters." I ponder that riddle as I wait for my turn. I go into the room with the imposing radiation machine, climb on the table, and put my hands over my head. The gown is slid down so the part to be radiated is exposed, and I am positioned accurately, thanks to the three tattoos. The techs leave the room, sliding the wide, heavy door until it clicks shut. Now it's just me and the radiation machine. It makes little clicking noises and moans like wind blowing past an open window. The table goes up and down and sideways, much like a tame carnival ride. Little parts open and shut behind the round glass of the x-ray machine as photons are pumped into my body. The machine swings under me and continues its work, photons passing thorough the table, which is made of carbon.

After ten minutes, the table is lowered, and I gratefully bring my arms down to my sides, am helped to stand, and leave. The techs are not only friendly but full of fun, which is why I wear crazy earrings when I come each day.

# BREATH AND BABIES

I am reading about breath as I eat breakfast on the patio among the flowers. "Each breath is a conversation with the environment in which something new is received and something old released." Thinking of breath this way takes me to an entirely different level, making the necessary act of breathing more creative and meaningful. I consciously breathe into the trees and bushes, the flowers, the soil and air around me. In the cool morning shade, I commune, a miraculous act, a giving and taking in.

Several summers ago, when we were in between cats, our yard became a day care center for young animals. I lost track of the number of baby birds who bumped and fluttered from ground to bush and back. A baby bunny decided to befriend us and spent the summer gazing Ferdinand-like at the flowers. Nothing was eaten, not even the vegetables in Dave's garden.

Now that Gia the huntress is in residence, birds and bunnies have wisely sought other facilities to care for their young; or so I thought. Last week, I found a baby robin perched on the railing of our porch. It had the typical cuteness of a baby bird, feather tufts on its head, and a fearless curiosity. "Get out of here," I cautioned. "A hunter cat lives here." The baby blinked and didn't move. "Where is your mommy?" I continued anxiously. It has been my observation that robins tend to be somewhat sloppy parents. Eventually, baby moved to a bush outside the window. Mama finally came along and tried to feed the baby a berry from the bush. "Stupid bird," I yelled. "Adult birds can barely get those berries down." As I said, robins are sloppy parents.

But wait, this morning I spot a baby phoebe perched on a pile of pruned branches near the driveway. "Fly up," I plead, my arms moving up and down to indicate up. The baby turns its head to look at me and then looks away, oblivious to my pleas. Eventually, two phoebes show up in the trees, and the next time I look, the baby is gone.

# BACK IN THE LAND OF GETTING THINGS DONE

Signs of illness are slowly disappearing. Dave puts the Tylenol away, and the cornstarch is back in the kitchen cupboard. I return my colored pencils and coloring book to the hobby box. I love coloring and have completed a shortened version of *Anne of Green Gables,* but now there is no time for that activity. I am back in the land of *getting things done.*

But having learned from my illness, I try to consider what is essential and what is not. I am getting better at being in the moment, at washing dishes to wash dishes instead of washing dishes to get done. I will continue to look for baby birds, look for the feathery tufts on their heads, and celebrate their beautiful innocence.

We are having guests. Grandsons Andrew and Eddie and their dad arrive just in time for a visit from Kyle's college friend Janie and her son, who are on vacation from Italy.

Sitting around the table, catching up after Janie's twenty-year absence from our lives, we are a diverse group representing a range of ages from Janie's seven-year-old son to seventy-seven-year-old David. Like the succession of flowers in our garden, we are budding, blooming, and fading, each representing a particular perspective, each unique.

Andrew and Eddie's week with us is filled with screams from the tire swing in the yard to sticky marshmallows roasted over an evening campfire. We consume copious amounts of summer food, ending with root beer sodas, duly photographed to join other photos in the family root beer soda archives (which go back to Todd and Kyle's toddler days). There are excursions through the glen, riotous swimming in the lake, and games played around the dining room table. I am on the periphery more than I wish due to the effects of radiology, including a nasty rash.

Now they are gone, and I bring up remembered pictures: Andrew's beautiful eyes, whose unfathomable depths hint of secrets, of mystery; curly-haired Eddie's smile, a joy, a welcoming, pure in intent.

There is barely enough time to change bedding before Todd and his wife Ariel arrive from Los Angeles. They are here for Todd's thirtieth high school reunion. Their visit is a flow of sound: hum of washer and dryer, slosh of dishwasher, gurgle of coffeepot. We are guided through computer games and YouTube offerings, and as always when Todd is around, we laugh a lot.

Now Dave and I ride through a perfect summer evening under majestic clouds, returning from the airport. The house, when we enter, greets us with perfect quiet. This is the experience of our children now: the joy of anticipated arrival, the bittersweet drive home after saying goodbye. "Sleep well, my darlings," I used to say, knowing they were secure under our roof and not a roof located miles away, as they are now. "Sleep well, my darlings," I continue to intone in my prayers.

# REACTION

I am a reactor. This is what my radiology doctor tells me as he surveys the rash that has developed on my chest and is spreading downward. "It will only get worse," he says gently. "You have eight more treatments, six of them focused on the most affected area. Hang in there." Apparently, this is the only advice he can give. I've gone through two kinds of ointment and am now on my third, called silver nitrate, which I slather on lavishly.

I look at my red skin tinged with purple. I envision scars. Not only am I discouraged, but I'm angry. I intend to hang in there, and I'll do it well. I'll be damned if I let this get me down.

The last phase of radiation is difficult and painful. It's like having bad sunburn and continuing to go out in the sun. The nurse has put a covering over the worst part, and ibuprofen helps with the pain. Lying on the couch under the ceiling fan with the area bared also helps.

I am in pain, and I am angry. The pain is from my reaction to radiation, which is probably due to the chemicals used in chemotherapy treatment. I can't help but wonder why better forms of treatment haven't been developed. Should one blindly accept that chemotherapy is the best way to treat cancer?

I hope for legislation that will encourage researchers to share their findings. I would ask for an attitude of hope and help for cancer victims instead of a profit margin. I envision better environmental checks. I wish medical marijuana was available in our state, in all states. Our local cancer center is very busy. My neighbor is dying of cancer. I am angry and feeling helpless.

# COMING BACK

I inch back into normalcy. Visiting my favorite breakfast restaurant, I am surprised to see everything is the same: the menu, the signs of specials on the wall, a poster advertising the upcoming St. Patrick's fair. Raffle tickets can be purchased in this restaurant as usual. I buy a set of six.

My hair is growing more and more. It looks like a crew cut, giving me a new persona, a boy in drag. My eyebrows are gone. I haven't lost all their hair, but the color is missing. My eyelashes, what is left of them, are also colorless. I've always had dark eyebrows and eyelashes. My skin is even more pale than usual. Will anyone recognize me? I can hardly recognize myself.

Early in the morning, David, Eileen, and I cross dew-drenched fields and tackle bushes pregnant with blueberries. Eileen, aware of my limited physical ability, donates her bucket to us, and we come away with a little over fourteen pounds of berries. Then we head back up over the hill to the next village for breakfast. Eileen and I are never sure if the high point of our annual blueberry excursion is the berries or the breakfast.

Near our breakfast restaurant is a small park where we took our children during the summer. Even now, as I stand by there, I can hear ghostly whoops and hollers from the Johnson clan as they jump on the stones lining the edge of the park before attacking their hamburgers and hot dogs. This was Kyle's first venture into the greater world when he was one week old. He sat atop a picnic table in his infant seat like a tiny king. *I'm still here,* I think, glancing around the park, *still making memories.*

# A DEATH

My neighbor Kurt is dead. We were not here when the hearse came to their home. We read about it in the paper, but the passage of time doesn't soften the blow. He was an outgoing, friendly neighbor, but my imagined bond with him was the disease we shared. He was my chemo buddy, and even though I knew his pancreatic cancer was probably terminal, I held out for a miracle. "You have a different kind of cancer. You don't have to worry about dying," his wife assures me at the funeral home when I burst into unwanted tears.

"He wasn't supposed to die," I blurt out. I should have died instead. I was older, had lived my life, and didn't have a young child depending on me. My mind is dark with that thought known as survivor's guilt.

"This is part of your own grieving process," I am reminded gently by my mentor. "Things have changed. Life has changed." A year ago, Dave said we were entering a new world. He was right.

# SUMMER'S END

This morning, I lay in bed listening to the rain. I haven't done that since I was a kid and free of responsibilities. "Are you going to sleep all day?" David asks from the bedroom doorway.

"Yes," I answer and pull the blanket up around my chin. I am lying in a position that is painless, and that comfort plus the soothing sheets of rain outside are just too delicious to give up. My mind wanders, and I think of our three children and the innocence of their early years. I was once mother, comforter, teacher, counselor. The children depended on their father and me. Now the tables are turning like a giant Ferris wheel that slowly switches the bottom wheel to the top and the top wheel down to the bottom. They are becoming, more and more, the comforters, counselors, and teachers we once were. I am no longer in charge. There is no better reminder of that than cancer. Yet while I mourn the loss of that role, I am aware of the soft sweetness of allowing others.

I regard the flowering plant on the patio. It looks dreadful. *How dare you?* I want to shout to the plant. *I've faithfully watered and fertilized you. How dare you?*

But this is the story at summer's end. Plants don't always cooperate. I wander the yard in my own late summer restlessness, thinking of how things change. There are no longer large toads in the gardens, killdeer no longer tease us with their fake wounded run, and the goldfinches stay in the fields away from the feeder. Even though the butterfly bushes are lush with blossoms, I have not seen a monarch butterfly, not one.

There are changes in us, also. We are not invincible. Illness has leaked in when we weren't looking. Our bodies aren't what they used to be. Our diets must change. This is the challenge. This is the time to live at the hub of the wheel, letting the rim rotate while we remain steady. This is the time to remember it's not what comes your way that's important: it's how you handle what comes.

This evening, Gia lopes around the corner of our house and jumps down by the cellar door, a bunny dangling limply from her mouth. David and I both yell at her, and the bunny drops to the ground, very much alive, and tries to climb the walls on either side of the walkway. "I'll get the cat, and you get the rabbit," Dave calls.

How does one *get* a frantic bunny? Feeling both terrified and helpless, I want to drop to the ground howling. David grabs Gia, and the bunny escapes into a bed of iris leaves.

I wish I could scream out the sadness locked within. I envy those who mourn loudly. My grief only sneaks out at night enmeshed in dark and heavy dreams. Needing solace, I walk through the damp fields, the thick grass a calming softness. Will there be fog later on? Crickets sing, synchronizing their late summer song as one pulsing chorus. Nothing stirs in the thick air. Leaves hang as if lifeless, and aside from the crickets, there is no sound. It is as if the universe has drawn in a breath and waits. What next? What next?

# WINDING DOWN

I am going everywhere without a head covering now. I no longer recognize the difference. No one stares or even seems to notice. My friend Eileen is right. People are too busy with their own thoughts to be aware of others.

Things seem to be coming to a close. My medicines are put away, borrowed wigs and hats returned, treatments over. A visit to my plastic surgeon confirms that she will not do a breast implant, as she thinks the flaps are too small, so I do not have a new chest after all. I am so happy that I won't have to have surgery that I forget about how awful I look. My oncologist puts the likelihood of cancer returning in the low to moderate range.

The skin on my chest is beginning to peel, and when I take off the transparent strips, I am aware of new skin underneath. The body renews itself in miraculous ways. My semi-annual checkup shows my health to be good despite being mowed by the chemo killer machine just months ago.

I show David a slight infection on my lower eyelid. "Good," he says with a smile. "Your immune system is working."

I am on a teeter-totter: the past is down and the future up, waiting for me to tip the way it is supposed to go. I have never been more aware of the fluidity, the dynamism of life: new skin, just beneath the surface, waiting to come into the light.

# PART THREE

## AFTERMATH

# A SCARE

It is an abscess, a simple tooth infection. My tooth had been sore on and off but not enough for a trip to the dentist. Then one day, a lump appears on my lower jaw. I make the appointment. Our dentist, once a pupil in my nursery school and a schoolmate of Suzanne's, is very kind. "I think it is an infection, but perhaps you should see your oncologist just in case," he says.

I go numb. Ambient sounds, hollow as if coming from underwater, float through my brain. Centering on the dentist's face with the intensity of a diamond drill, I try to appear calm. I continue the conversation, agreeing to call my oncologist, wondering what I will say to David. I check carefully for clues from his expression to see if my dentist is worried. He too appears calm, his face expressionless.

I call for an appointment with my oncologist. Could I come that afternoon? Lumps appearing on the body of one who has had cancer are akin to chest pains in a cardiac patient. Everyone springs into action.

My oncologist thinks it is probably an infection but—"Just to be sure; you know how thorough I am"—schedules a CAT scan and bone scan. "We've been through a lot together," he says and, instead of giving me the usual handshake as he leaves the examining room, hugs me, leaving warmth in the midst of cold possibilities.

Back to the hospital I go, dutifully putting on the hospital gown, drinking the fluid, and having the injection. *I can do this. I've done it before. I'm feeling positive. I am okay.* I smile and joke with the nurse. I am witty.

The tests are easy, almost comfortable. But as my narrow bed is wheeled out of the scanner, I suddenly see an image of myself with my defenses slathered over my body like dried mud. Cracks appear on the surface, snaking this way and that. The cracks slowly break away, falling to my feet, leaving me alone, naked, and vulnerable. I leave the hospital with only one thought in mind: *I have to get home.* Once there, I sit on the couch. "I want to stay here," I say numbly. "I can't go anywhere." We cancel a meeting we are to attend that evening.

The next day, David and I go to have our blood tests in preparation for our semi-annual checkup. The facility is located across from the hospital complex. I look at the sprawl of buildings and immediately have a panic attack.

"What's going on?" I tearfully ask my spiritual guide, who sits next to me in our living room, holding my hand.

"You are most likely experiencing post-traumatic stress," she replies quietly.

"But I haven't been in a war."

"Yes, you have," she says. "You have been through a lot. This is the residue."

"Collateral damage," I answer, trying a weak laugh.

"Exactly," she says, shaking her head in agreement. "You have also been given many gifts."

I nod, thinking of all the lessons I have learned. "But the most important gift is being stripped of your defenses," she continues. "Cancer is the great opener. With your defenses gone, your authenticity arises. It is no longer covered up. You know, when we finally face God, we do so alone and with nothing."

I look around the quiet room and sigh. Her words comfort and reassure me, but I know this is not over. The only way out of this dark nightmare of fear and dread is to go through it: not over, under, or around, but through. I know this intellectually, but experiencing it is an entirely different matter.

The following days and weeks are bleak, my outlook one of despair rather than hope. I feel like a river ice jam, wishing I could cry, wishing for release, even clarity.

The cancer that I refused to fear has brought me to my knees.

# TRANSFORMATION

I surrender. I pull my last few fingers from the grip of holding and fall into the darkness of vulnerability.

Defenseless, I must accept what comes, not what I manufacture. I had hoped this experience would transform my former self into a new, more perfect me. In other words, I had fought to be in control. In doing this, I had really been trying to beat the disease after all.

Cancer sliced through my life with a razor-edged sword, leaving two parts: before and after. Before is what was and no longer is, and after doesn't look so good. I have aged. My skin has new wrinkles, and my eyebrows are no longer thick and dark. I don't have the strength I once had. My memory is impaired. I'm not who I thought I was.

Happily, I am *not* who I thought I was. Stepping out of the battered remains of my defended self, I am more ready to say yes to God's will without trying to script his response.

I had not expected to be vulnerable, but in vulnerability I find a place not dark but rich in blessing. I sought an ending, a certificate of survival. But there is no *finis.* One does not get over cancer or the subsequent treatments. One gets through it. The way is long and painful, yet it is a journey of discovery, of gifts, of healing. Here in this new evolution, I set my steps in the next direction.

"This being human is a guest house. Every morning a new arrival."

"Welcome," I say with outstretched arms. "Come in."

# WHAT CAN YOU DO FOR A FRIEND WHO HAS CANCER?

Flowers (but only if your friend can care for them)
A gift card for a massage
A gift card for acupuncture
Mouthwash for dry mouth
ChapStick
Lotion for dry skin
Cornstarch
A soft fleece blanket
A knit cap
Cheery get well cards sent frequently
Colorful balloons
A prepaid card to your friend's favorite coffee shop
Backrubs and foot massages
Sit with him/her quietly
Listen

# ACKNOWLEDGMENTS

For David: You are my friend, my lover, my hero. Your patience and care have been saintly.

For Kelly, my princess of mercy, who cooked, cleaned, manicured, pedicured, soothed, and cheered.

For Joel: Without you, this book would not have been possible.

For Matthew, who came to visit and sent beautiful flowers.

For Claudia, who ran for me and pulled me along in my journey.

For Zaynab, my spiritual rock, who teaches me again and again what love looks like.

For Wadud, who called every day and said, "How are you doing?"

For Linda, who probably saved my life and kept me going with cards and gifts.

For the Tuesday study group: you nurture my mind, body, and spirit.

For the Sufi Order of Rochester, who showed love in so many wonderful ways.

For my friends, who carried me along, and for Caring Bridge, which provided a vehicle for our connection.

For Quiet Meadows, where I have been nurtured and taught by nature all these years.

For *The Ellen DeGeneres Show*, which made me laugh when I thought laughter was no longer possible.

For all medical personnel, whose expertise and care found the cancer, cut it away, and hopefully scared it from coming back.

CPSIA information can be obtained at www.ICGtesting.com
Printed in the USA
BVOW04s1959251114

376721BV00001B/2/P